PREFACE

I n this world of uncertain times, we search for answers to life's problems. Poverty, racism, religious factions, global pandemics, natural disasters, political division, substance abuse, wars, and financial crisis are just a few examples of the issues that plague us. In the face of all this, we wonder, *Is there a God and does he seem to care?* The answer—at least, in my mind—is, yes, there is a God, and he does care. What a topic for me to tackle. Are these all signs of what the Bible describes as signs of the end times? If so, why does it matter?

I was very fortunate as a child to have a grandmother, Mary Francis Schrum, who had a great faith in God. She was not overtly religious; however, everyone who knew her knew she was a woman of faith by the love that she shared. As she taught me about the Bible, I was influenced by her love to have faith in Christ, and I accepted him as my Lord and Savior. Since then, I have met many other humble people in my life who influenced my faith the way my grandmother did.

As I read through the Bible, I saw flawed individuals throughout the Scriptures who had very little education and a low social status, who went on to accomplish great things for God and for humanity. I also saw people of great education and status whom God humbled and used mightily for his purpose. As God began to open my eyes, I saw people around me who were like the people in the Scriptures. I was deeply influenced by a number of leaders who followed Christ. I heard leaders like Billy Graham, Charles Stanley, T. D. Jakes, Joyce Myers, and many others teach the Bible. Many of their testimonies are powerful; they came from humble beginnings and went on to impact the world for Christ.

I had mentors in my life who would seem to be unlikely candidates for the job. I had a father-in-law who was an unbeliever who taught me how to succeed in business and encouraged me to get an education. I had a college professor who taught me that ministry is not about fame or fortune but humbly serving others. I was ordained and selected for a regional jail ministry. I taught Bible studies for years prior to that. I was asked to help a friend pastor a church. I did evangelism work in the inner city and preached at many of the churches in that area. I went on to start a ministry and pastor a church for years. The entire focus of all these ministries was to help the hurting, the lost, and those in poverty transform their lives. As I ministered to others, God was using all this to educate me in what true ministry is. I hope to pass on some of the lessons I learned from the leaders who influenced me.

The greatest influence on my life was the life and ministry of Jesus. Can we believe that the one who led humble fishermen and sinners to God is still relevant today? He was able to lead people to transcend themselves. He provided prophetic insight and brought about the highest level of change not just in his generation but for all eternity. Because of the great paradigm shift that we are going through today with advanced technology—the Internet, social media, and many other advancements in information—we need Jesus Christ to enable us to go beyond our own selfish desires to empower us to be more than we have been. The Bible communicates a compelling vision for our lives and for the future.

Perhaps you are looking for answers to some of life's problems, and you believe there is more to life than you are experiencing. So if you are searching for God, how do you find him? If you are looking for answers, where do you find them? Are you destined for greatness and possibly missing out on the call that God has on your life? If we could simply see ourselves through the eyes of God instead of looking to our own failures and imperfections and selfhoods, we could live for him and impart a vision to the next generation.

Jesus of Nazareth was the greatest leader in the history of the world. What set him apart from what we consider great leaders? Presidents and kings call on him for help in their leadership. Ministers and rabbis teach his principles. His ability to heal the brokenhearted, to bind up our wounds, and to set us free are just a few of the reasons why we worship him. The fact that he is the way, the truth, the life, and the door to eternal life is a more important reason to adore him.

These topics are nothing new for mankind; as a matter of fact, Jesus taught all these principles. It would seem that society has turned away from loving his neighbor, treating the least of these as a child of God, and healing the hurting and lost. I thought it best to examine what Christ actually taught compared to what we sometimes hear today. The church seems afraid to tackle these very important principles for fear of retribution or reprisal.

Jesus was marginalized. He was poor, powerless by his own choice, misunderstood, maligned, arrested, tortured, and murdered. Jesus broke conventional rules of polite Jewish religious society. He associated with prostitutes and tax collectors. He touched the bodies of lepers and the corpses of the deceased. He interacted with and uplifted women, children, peasants, the infirm, the mentally ill, and Gentiles.

The church today works very hard to be accepted by its surrounding society rather than being the kind of Christians taught about in the Bible. Many congregations of the contemporary church strive to blend with society to be appealing. Jesus engaged people of other faiths who lived all around him. He related to Samaritans, Romans, other Gentiles, and those who seemed to follow no religious path, yet he did so with compassion, respect, and cooperation. Alternately, the church today is often fearful, suspicious, judgmental, and unloving toward persons who are not Christians. They treat the religious other as targets for evangelism but not as neighbors and friends.

Jesus focused on loving and forgiving more than on doctrinal orthodoxy. John 14:6 has Jesus claiming to be "the way, the truth, and the life." The "way" is a compassionate way, a manner of living, a pathway that one walks and not just a doorway into heaven. That's why the earliest believers were known by others as followers of the way.

On his journey both inside and outside of Palestine, Jesus walked a merciful way. He healed the frightened woman who was hemorrhaging blood and was desperately weakened and hopeless but was bold enough to risk a crowd's censure and touch the mysterious stranger's cloak. He asked Zacchaeus to give back money he had extorted and then shocked everyone by going home for dinner at the tax collector's house. He forgave the woman caught in adultery and stopped her from being stoned to death by self-righteous male accusers. Jesus himself led a small congregation of men and women who were growing deeper in their understanding and love in their walk with him. Maybe to be that kind of church, we should rethink some aspects of our community life so we can respond to people's felt needs more genuinely. This, I believe, is truly the love of Christ.

I examine the Scriptures and reveal what Jesus taught about many of the problems we have in the world today. These issues are nothing new in the history of mankind. When we forget the problems of the past and where to turn for answers, we tend to repeat our mistakes. Jesus teaches us about all the issues we face today and the culmination of all this. However, one cannot be truly prepared to experience the end of days without knowing God. This means placing one's trust in God, believing in the resurrection of his son, and confessing Jesus as Lord (Romans 10:9–13). Even in the face of calamity and persecution, the believer has hope in the coming of Christ in his glory and spending an eternity with him in a way that the nonbeliever does not. To be free from the power of sin and death and be made in the newness of life and be hopeful of the resurrection to come, we must first take Jesus at his word:

> Heaven and earth shall pass away, but my words shall not pass away. (Matthew 24:35)

ACKNOWLEDGMENTS

I wish to thank my grandmother, Mary Francis Schrum, for the godly influence she displayed as an example for me and everyone around her. She had a great faith in God. She was not overtly religious; however, everyone who knew her knew she was a woman of faith by the love that she shared. She taught me the Scriptures by the way that she lived. She treated everyone she met as if they were family. She would greet a stranger on the street as if they were old friends. She talked to homeless people to encourage them and give away her last change to make a difference. Her coworkers, church family, family, and friends all looked up to her. They admired her not for what she had; they admired her for who she was.

I would like thank Joan and Earl Ketcham, two godly parents and grandparents and leaders in the church, who taught me how to love others unconditionally. They treated me as if I were their own son and supported me in my years in the ministry. Joan is a woman who seeks God with all her heart, and even though she has faced great trials in her life, she never wavered in her faith. Her humble heart and simple prayers and loving conversations changed the lives of many young women. Earl was a father figure to many young men who did not have that influence in their life.

As a leader in the church, Hilda Myrick reached out with a hug and kind, loving words when I was questioning my direction in life. She was a woman who was full of the Holy Spirit and wisdom from God. She was a leader in the church we attended and truly lived for Christ as an example to others. I was busy in business and attending college and wondered if I had time for God. When this little old lady, after church one Sunday, gave me a hug and said "I love you," it melted my hard heart. I knew at that moment that I needed God more than all the other things that I was seeking after.

My friend Alan McColl keeps me grounded in the faith and has overcome so much in his life. He is an inspiration to me and lives his life for God and Christ in a very humble way. If you were to ask him, he would say that he is far from perfect. In reality, others can see that he loves God, his family, and his friends with all his heart. Al strives to perform work, family, and ministry with excellence.

To my loving wife, Belinda, whom God has transformed the life and heart of, she prays for me constantly. God answers her very humble prayers in such a gentle way. Her faith in God and me is an inspiration. The way that she ministers to the lost, the hurting, and the hungry impacts the lives of others in a way that I have rarely seen in life or in church. She would choose to feed the hungry and purchase clothes for the poor rather than buying something for herself. It is her compassion and love that touches the hearts of others.

THE WOMAN AT THE WELL

This Gospel episode is referred to as a paradigm for our engagement with truth in the Roman Curia book, a Christian reflection on the New Age, as the dialogue says: "You worship what you do not know; we worship what we know." And it offers an example of "Jesus Christ the bearer of the water of life." The passages that comprise John 4:10–26 are sometimes referred to as the water of life discourse, which forms a complement to the bread of life discourse.

The story about Jesus and the woman at the well found in John 4:4–42 illustrates what God thinks about religious people. He met a Samaritan woman at the well around twelve in the afternoon. The Jews looked down on Samaritans. They considered them a mixed-breed people, and even though they worshipped the same God and used similar Scriptures, they accused one another of not worshipping correctly. In addition, women in that society would not have been spoken to as an equal to men. Jesus prophesied to the woman about her past. He told her that she had had multiple marriages and was now living with a man. During that time, she would automatically be condemned by Jewish law. Jesus had a conversation with her about her past and about the divisions between the Jewish and Samaritan religions and told the woman he was the Christ, the Messiah described in the Scriptures. The woman went into town and told the towns people that this man was the Christ. The town's people came out to hear him and were convinced for themselves that he was, indeed, the Christ. A large portion of the town then followed Jesus and his teachings. They invited him to stay, and he agreed to stay for two more days.

His demonstration here is that we are all on the same level when it comes to salvation and eternal life; he shows that no one is above others in the eyes of God. He shows us that religion is not the answer; rather, it is a relationship with Christ and a repentant heart (a change of mind leading to a change of actions) that leads us to salvation. He shows us that living for him and submitting ourselves to the work of the Holy Spirit is what transforms our life and our attitudes toward God and humanity. Jesus is making an evangelistic journey to show his disciples that the Gospel is for all people.

Now let's examine the Scriptures in John 4:4–42.

> Now he had to go through Samaria. So he came to a town in Samaria called Sychar, near the plot of ground Jacob had given to his son Joseph. Jacob's well was there, and Jesus, tired as he was from the journey, sat down by the well. It was about noon.
>
> When a Samaritan woman came to draw water, Jesus said to her, "Will you give

me a drink?" (His disciples had gone into the town to buy food.)

The Samaritan woman said to him, "You are a Jew and I am a Samaritan woman. How can you ask me for a drink?" (For Jews do not associate with Samaritans.

Jesus answered her, "If you knew the gift of God and who it is that asks you for a drink, you would have asked him and he would have given you living water."

"Sir," the woman said, "you have nothing to draw with and the well is deep. Where can you get this living water? Are you greater than our father Jacob, who gave us the well and drank from it himself, as did also his sons and his livestock?"

Jesus answered, "Everyone who drinks this water will be thirsty again, but whoever drinks the water I give them will never thirst. Indeed, the water I give them will become in them a spring of water welling up to eternal life."

The woman said to him, "Sir, give me this water so that I won't get thirsty and have to keep coming here to draw water."

He told her, "Go, call your husband and come back."

"I have no husband," she replied.

Jesus said to her, "You are right when you say you have no husband. The fact is, you have had five husbands, and the man you now have is not your husband. What you have just said is quite true."

"Sir," the woman said, "I can see that you are a prophet. Our ancestors worshiped on this mountain, but you Jews claim that the place where we must worship is in Jerusalem."

"Woman," Jesus replied, "believe me, a time is coming when you will worship the Father neither on this mountain nor in Jerusalem. You Samaritans worship what you do not know; we worship what we do know, for salvation is from the Jews. Yet a time is coming and has now come when the true worshipers will worship the Father in the Spirit and in truth, for they are the kind of worshipers the Father seeks. God is spirit, and his worshipers must worship in the Spirit and in truth."

The woman said, "I know that Messiah" (called Christ) "is coming. When he comes, he will explain everything to us."

Then Jesus declared, "I, the one speaking to you—I am he."

The Disciples Rejoin Jesus

Just then his disciples returned and were surprised to find him talking with a woman. But no one asked, "What do you want?" or "Why are you talking with her?"

Then, leaving her water jar, the woman went back to the town and said to the people, "Come, see a man who told me everything I ever did. Could this be the Messiah?" They came out of the town and made their way toward him.

Meanwhile his disciples urged him, "Rabbi, eat something."

But he said to them, "I have food to eat that you know nothing about."

Then his disciples said to each other, "Could someone have brought him food?"

"My food," said Jesus "is to do the will of him who sent me and to finish his work. Don't you have a saying, 'It's still four months until harvest'? I tell you, open your eyes and look at the fields! They are ripe for harvest. Even now the one who reaps draws a wage and harvests a crop for eternal life, so that the sower and the reaper may be glad together. Thus, the saying 'One sows and another reaps' is true. I sent you to reap what you have not worked for. Others have done the hard work, and you have reaped the benefits of their labor."

Many Samaritans Believe

Many of the Samaritans from that town believed in him because of the woman's testimony, "He told me everything I ever did." So when the Samaritans came to him, they urged him to stay with them, and he stayed two days. And because of his words many more became believers.

They said to the woman, "We no longer believe just because of what you said; now we have heard for ourselves, and we know that this man really is the Savior of the world."

So let's unpack the story.

The woman at the well was a Samaritan. So what does the story mean to us and what is Jesus trying to convey to us? Jews of the northern kingdom of Israel intermarried with the Assyrians and produced what the Jews considered a half-Jewish, half-Gentile Samaritan race.

As a result, the two groups had nothing to do with each other. This is ironic because Abraham, the father of the Jewish faith and Christianity and considered to be father of the Jews and Arabs, was thought to be born in Ur of Chaldees, modern day southern Iraq. He moved to Haran, modern day Turkey, before moving on to Canaan, modern Israel. His descendants were forced to migrate to Egypt and kept as slaves for approximately four hundred years. One of Abraham's descendants, Moses, married an Ethiopian woman, showing us that Israel and a Jewish nation were formed by a multinational, multiracial people whom God had called to be his own people. They were chosen by God. Ironically enough, we still face racial and religious discrimination even today. Sometimes, there is as much discrimination in the church as in the world. Jesus is showing us that we need to put those divisions aside and love one another unconditionally as he loves us.

Jesus was at Jacob's well and asked the Samaritan woman for a drink. The Bible gives the time of about twelve in the afternoon. Women of that time were considered more like property and had no rights in society. The woman had been in multiple relationships and was living with a man who was not her husband. Jesus brought that to her attention; I believe he wanted her to know that even though the religious leaders of the day and society would condemn her, he came through God's grace to forgive her. Most of the women would have gone out early in the cool of morning to draw water from the well. Was this woman shunned by the woman of that day making her ashamed to interact with them? Why did Jesus pick this woman to minister to? I believe more people would attend church and seek God if they simply knew that God accepts them just like they are. He wants us to come to him and confess that we are sinners so that he can transform our lives.

She was perplexed that Jesus would have a conversation with a Samaritan woman. She probably thought that like many others, all Jews hated Samaritans. They had a conversation about what true religion was. The Samaritans saw themselves as the keepers of the Torah and had their own unique copy of the Pentateuch (the first five books of Moses). They had a unique religious system and worshipped on Mount Gerizim; they considered the Jerusalem temple and Levitical system illegitimate. The Jews thought that their religious system was the only way to worship God and that the Samaritans had it wrong. That sounds a lot like our religious denominations and churches today. We think we have all the answers in our traditions and the way that we worship and minister. The truth is that we have part of the answer and that variation in churches makes room for all kinds of people to worship. The stories in the Scriptures, like this one, are important for us to learn from. Jesus illustrates the importance of not judging others for what they believe or what they have done.

Jesus stated to the woman that salvation was of the Jews. He explained to her that he was a descendant of the Jews and that salvation would come through him and not a religious system either in Samaria or Jerusalem and that salvation was for the whole world through him. She did not know that he was revealing to her that he would die for her sins and be resurrected for all mankind. His disciples would go on with his teachings and form the church and transform the world. They only knew at this time that he was a great prophet and that he had performed great miraculous signs. They did not know he was the Christ at this point. So why did Jesus pick this woman to reveal himself as Messiah? Jesus was showing his disciples that salvation was for all races, nations, cultures, and peoples. Most importantly, he was offering eternal salvation to a woman who would be rejected by the religious system of that day. The Bible says that we are not saved by what we do; rather, we are saved by confessing that Jesus Christ is Lord and then receiving him in our hearts. At that point, we are accepted into the kingdom of God and are given the Holy Spirit to transform us, and if we allow, then God will do the transformation in us by changing our desires.

The woman went back to her town and told everyone what Jesus said and proclaimed him as Messiah. The woman who once was ashamed was now forgiven and preaching Christ to the people. She essentially became the very first evangelist; as a result, many of the townspeople came out to hear Jesus teach. And they also proclaimed him as the Messiah, the Savior of the world described in the Old Testament Scriptures. The woman proclaimed that this man told her everything she ever did; she knew that God was looking directly in her heart and loved her just like she was. She possibly felt the unconditional love of God for the first time in her life. God knows who we are and what we do, yet he accepts us just the way that we are.

Jesus began to teach the other townspeople, and they also received eternal salvation because of his words. At the same time that he was teaching the Samaritans, he was teaching his own chosen disciples. He was teaching them to love people unconditionally and to simply accept them and let them know that God through his son was reaching out beyond the walls of the synagogue. His disciples were fishermen, tax collectors, prostitutes, and common everyday people. I believe he chose these people for the same reason that he ministered to the Samaritan woman: to show us that salvation was not just for the religious and social elite but for all mankind. Yes, the Gospel is for all mankind; however, God demonstrates in the Scriptures that he is against pious, pretentious, religious people who assume they have all the answers. These humble disciples of Jesus went on to become great leaders in the church and turned the world upside down for God.

He began to minister to the woman about the Holy Spirit. Jesus told the woman that if she drank the water from Jacob's well, she would thirst again; but if she drank the water he had to offer, she would never thirst again. She asked him for some of that water. He went on to tell her that God was a spirit and those who worshipped him must worship him in spirit and in truth. Jesus was teaching her that it was the Holy Spirit, the living water from God, that filled us, and that was what she needed. The Bible teaches us that salvation is a transformation that takes place from the inside out. Once we accept Christ as Lord and Savior, the Holy Spirit comes to reside in us to help us live for God. But much like the woman at the well described in this story, we need to accept Christ, confess our sins, and worship God to stir up the Holy Spirit in us, thus quenching our spiritual thirst. We accomplish this by having fellowship with other believers, praising God in worship, and praying and studying the Scriptures. The Bible says that this is a formula for living a successful Christian life.

Jesus taught his disciples about a harvest of the fields, meaning, the harvest of people for eternal life. He said we would reap where we did not sow. So what does Jesus mean by that? He stated that the religious system of that day, even though it was flawed, set the foundation of his coming and of the church. He also stated that the church was flawed with man-made rules and regulations and imperfect people but that it was still the instrument that he worked through. What he is illustrating is that true evangelism is preaching the Gospel to mankind so we will reap a harvest of souls for eternal life. You may have experienced the same thing when someone told you about being a Christian and invited you to church and a pastor or teacher taught a sermon that impacted your life. After that, you went out and told someone about Christ and, as a result, won a soul to the kingdom of God. Jesus tells us in the Bible to go into the entire world and preach the Gospel to the entire world and to all peoples. In this Scripture, he is demonstrating this directly to his disciples and showing us how to do that.

The Scriptures say, "Blessed and fortunate and happy and spiritually prosperous (in that state in which the born-again child of God enjoys his favor and salvation) are those who hunger and thirst for righteousness (uprightness and right standing with God) for they shall be completely satisfied!" It means to hunger and thirst for justice is to have a strong and continuous desire of a religious lifestyle and high moral standards. It is someone who wants what is right just as much as another who is dying of thirst wants a glass of water.

THE ADULTEROUS WOMAN

Jesus and the woman taken in adultery (often called pericope adulterae, for short) is a passage (pericope) found in the Gospel of John 7:53 to 8:11 that has been the subject of much scholarly discussion.

In this story, Jesus is showing that God's love is for everyone, even those who have fallen from grace. Jewish law stated that a woman caught in the act of adultery must be put to death. The Jewish leaders tested Jesus to see if he would go against the Law of Moses. Jesus admonished those who were without sin to cast the first stone. One by one, they all walked away, and only the woman remained. Jesus asked her if anyone had condemned her. She replied that they had not. He told her that he had forgiven her as well. The men of the city were so caught up in the sin that she committed that they failed to recognize their own guilt. This is a story of God's forgiveness and unfailing love.

Let's read the Scriptures in John 8:1–11.

> But Jesus went to the Mount of Olives.
>
> At dawn he appeared again in the temple courts; where all the people gathered around him, and he sat down to

teach them. The teachers of the law and the Pharisees brought in a woman caught in adultery. They made her stand before the group and said to Jesus, "Teacher, this woman was caught in the act of adultery. In the Law Moses commanded us to stone such women. Now what do you say?" They were using this question as a trap, in order to have a basis for accusing him.

But Jesus bent down and started to write on the ground with his finger. When they kept on questioning him, he straightened up and said to them, "Let any one of you who is without sin be the first to throw a stone at her." Again he stooped down and wrote on the ground.

At this, those who heard began to go away one at a time, the older ones first, until only Jesus was left, with the woman still standing there. Jesus straightened up and asked her, "Woman, where are they? Has no one condemned you?"

"No one, sir," she said.

"Then neither do I condemn you," Jesus declared. "Go now and leave your life of sin."

There Is No Condemnation to Those Who Are in Christ

In the passage, Jesus was teaching in the Second Temple after coming from the Mount of Olives. A group of scribes and Pharisees confronted Jesus, interrupting his teaching. They brought in a woman, accusing her of committing adultery, claiming she was caught in the very act. They told Jesus that the punishment for someone like her should be stoning, as prescribed by Mosaic Law. Jesus began to write something on the ground using his finger. But when the woman's accusers continued their challenge, he stated that the one who was without sin was the one who should cast the first stone at her. The accusers and congregants (church people) departed, realizing not one of them was without sin either, leaving Jesus alone with the woman. Jesus asked the woman if anyone had condemned her, and she answered no. Jesus said that he too did not condemn her and told her to go and sin no more. This was a story of God's redemption and love.

So let us analyze this story a little closer.

Jesus is showing us that when we are condemned by sin or feel condemned by other people and what they perceive us to be, we simply need to turn to God to forgive us. Yes, under their law, given by God to Moses, she would have been condemned to certain death. The religious leaders failed to recognize that they also had sin in their life and the consequences they could face as a result. They were teaching the law to others and failing to live by it themselves. Jesus knew this and intended to teach them a lesson. Not only did he intend to teach the leaders a lesson but he also intended to overturn the corrupt legal system of that day. He was showing that true justice should be administered fairly and not just pointed at one person that the leaders thought worthy to condemn. What about the man that she was caught with? Why was he not found guilty of the same moral wrong? Was the judicial system prejudiced?

What was Jesus writing in the sand? One can only speculate what he was writing. My guess is that he was spelling out their names one by one to get their attention. God knows us and the intention of our hearts; we would rather point a finger at someone else for doing wrong rather than confront our own sin. The Bible says that he stood up; I believe he was looking at them in the eye, knowing their deception. Imagine that: God looking at you directly in the eye and calling your bluff. The lawyers of that day had written their own regulations into the law to benefit themselves, and the lawyers were using it for their own personal gain. Then the Bible says that he stooped down again and began writing again. Was he possibly writing a list of their sins under the names that he had just written? Jesus, the Scriptures say, ignored the accusations hurled at the women by the religious and social leaders. The purpose of them testing Jesus was simply meant to interrupt his teaching, which he totally ignored.

This sounds a lot like our legal system today. People are suing people just to get wealthy at the expense of others. We have a legal system that benefits the wealthy and well educated and discriminates against people who really need justice. Similarly, we have an educational system designed to indoctrinate the masses to achieve a social engineering objective with rules that were not followed by the professors (Pharisees). They had a government system designed to control the lives of the multitude at the expense of a lower class of citizens to reap benefits for themselves. They lived under a set of religious rules that were intended for subordinates to follow while ignored by the ruling class. Jesus was calling them out on all their hypocrisy. Jesus is showing us through this teaching that true righteousness is found only through God's forgiveness and not the rules of others. The legal system can be fair at times, and it helps regulate our society; however, when it is corrupt, there is no justice at all.

The Scriptures also state that they were trying to trap him in his own words. They did not realize that this was God speaking directly to them. They thought they would simply trip him up in his message to get him to leave them alone. He was disrupting their lives and their ability to control the people. Who did this man think he was challenging their legal system and siding with this woman? Imagine that these men were trying to manipulate God and outsmart him with their own self-righteous objections. Have you ever tried to justify your own wrong by saying it was the fault of another? The Bible says that we are to judge our own actions. Treating others wrong just because they are wrong does not solve an error. Rather, reflecting on why we are wrong and rising above it is the right action.

Jesus is showing us that his forgiveness is far greater than our earthly legal system. He is also showing us that his legal system is for all mankind regardless of how high people hold themselves in their own esteem. We are all the same in God's eyes and will all face his judgment. The Bible says that judgment will be administered based on the way that we judge others. The Bible clearly states that we cannot be forgiven by God unless we are willing to completely forgive others of the wrong or the perceived wrong they have done to us. We have to trust God that he is able to vindicate us and judge rightly. He alone is worthy to resolve injustice in this world and the world to come. So our justification for eternal life will not be based on the good that we have done on earth but simply that we needed a God to forgive us for the wrong that we have done. That frees us up to simply rest in the assurance that God will take care of us in this life and to know for certain that we have eternal life.

The Scriptures say that they all dropped the stones that they were going to use for capital punishment and that they all walked away. Jesus had silenced his critics. A new system of justice was being taught by Jesus. Jesus was administering a fair system that would endure through eternity. A system that says, "God sent his only begotten son to die for our sins so that we would not be condemned but forgiven." This is a system that says that it is only us who can condemn ourselves, not God and not others. The Bible says that God does not reject us but that he loves us. We reject God when we turn away from him and follow our own selfish desires.

The woman no longer felt condemned. Was she, in a time of weakness, looking for attention? Was she possibly condemned by society because of her past and looking for any means necessary to fill the desires she had for companionship? We really do not know the answer, but whatever the reason, she was forgiven and given a new start by God. What could her critics say now? The Bible teaches us that we are not to get caught up in what others think of us but to live right lives and leave the consequences to God. What a wonderful feeling to be fully forgiven and to no longer to have to feel ashamed.

I hear stories of young women and even young men getting caught up in the images and messages portrayed by others on social media and in other medias. This creates a poor self-image and can lead to anorexia and other illnesses. It can lead to substance abuse and other self-defeating behaviors. It can also cause us to want to feel loved by others and lead to relationships much like the woman in this story. We think we have to live up to all those images portrayed to us by television and social media.

In reality, most of the people in the images we see are hurting too and are looking for the same answers that I am describing here. Even though they may seem to have it all together, they need God too! We need to embrace who God created each of us to be and feel good about ourselves. Stop worrying about what others think, develop a positive self-image, and enjoy the outcome regardless of what anyone thinks. We cannot have a healthy relationship without allowing others to embrace themselves and encourage them to be all that God created them to be. We can only do that if we love ourselves as God loves us. Jesus does not condemn the woman in the story but condemns the behavior of the ones who are judging her.

The Scriptures say do not judge or you too will be judged. For in the same way you judge others, you will be judged, and with the measure you use, it will be measured to you. "Why do you look at the speck of sawdust in your brother's eye and pay no attention to the plank in your own eye?" If we're really going to obey this command (and it is a pretty clear command), we need to change our own hearts. We need to remember that we are sinners ourselves. We have done wrong. We mess up every day. Thus, we need to have compassion on others who have done wrong.

THE PRODIGAL SON

The parable of the prodigal son (also known as the parable of the two brothers, lost son, loving father, or the forgiving father) is one of the parables of Jesus in the Bible, appearing in Luke 15:11–32. Jesus shares the parable with his disciples, the Pharisees, and others.

In the story, a father has two sons. The younger son asks for his portion of inheritance from his father, who grants his son's request. This son, however, is prodigal (i.e., wasteful and extravagant), thus squandering his fortune by living a party lifestyle and eventually becoming destitute (broke). As a consequence, he now must return home empty-handed and intend to beg his father to accept him back as a servant. To the son's surprise, he is not scorned by his father but is welcomed back with celebration and a welcoming party. Envious, the older son refuses to participate in the festivities. The father tells the older son: "You are ever with me, and all that I have is yours, but thy younger brother was lost and now he is found." This is a story of a father's love for his children and a desire for their restoration.

Let's see what the Scriptures have to say in Luke 15:11–32.

The Parable of the Lost Son

Jesus continued: "There was a man who had two sons. The younger one said to his father, 'Father, give me my share of the estate.' So he divided his property between them.

"Not long after that, the younger son got together all he had, set off for a distant country and there squandered his wealth in wild living. After he had spent everything, there was a severe famine in that whole country, and he began to be in need. So he went and hired himself out to a citizen of that country, who sent him to his fields to feed pigs. He longed to fill his stomach with the pods that the pigs were eating, but no one gave him anything.

"When he came to his senses, he said, 'How many of my father's hired servants have food to spare, and here I am starving to death! I will set out and go back to my father and say to him: Father, I have sinned against heaven and against you. I am no longer worthy to be called your son; make me like one of your hired servants.' So he got up and went to his father.

"But while he was still a long way off, his father saw him and was filled with compassion for him; he ran to his son, threw his arms around him and kissed him.

"The son said to him, 'Father, I have sinned against heaven and against you. I am no longer worthy to be called your son.'

"But the father said to his servants, 'Quick! Bring the best robe and put it on him. Put a ring on his finger and sandals on his feet. Bring the fattened calf and kill it. Let's have a feast and celebrate. For this son of mine was dead and is alive again; he was lost and is found.' So they began to celebrate.

"Meanwhile, the older son was in the field. When he came near the house, he heard music and dancing. So he called one of the servants and asked him what was going on. 'Your brother has come,' he replied, 'and your father has killed the fattened calf because he has him back safe and sound.'

"The older brother became angry and refused to go in. So his father went out and pleaded with him. But he answered his father, 'Look! All these years I've been slaving for you and never disobeyed your orders. Yet you never gave me even a young goat so I could celebrate with my friends. But when this son of yours who

has squandered your property with prostitutes comes home, you kill the fattened
calf for him!'

"'My son,' the father said, 'you are
always with me, and everything I have
is yours. But we had to celebrate and be
glad, because this brother of yours was
dead and is alive again; he was lost and is
found.'"

The story narrative

This story is a parable told by Jesus and demonstrates
the love of God toward people who stray away from him.
It is also a story of an older brother who demonstrates the
church and Christians who think that they do not need
God's continual forgiveness. Jesus was demonstrating by
the young man squandering all his money and taking a job
feeding the pigs that he had hit an all-time low. Pigs in that
time were not considered clean to eat, and they lived in
filth. The Bible says that the young man realized that even
the servants in his father's house were living better than
him. It's true that church is not perfect and there are hypocrites, but there are godly people who care and want you to
have God's best. The servants represent Christians, and the
father's house represents the church. The father is God, and
the jealous son is representative of a Christian with a wrong
attitude toward his fellow man.

How many times do we hear of a young man raised
in a good home who turned away to party and "just have

fun"? Or maybe a young man who grew up in a home without a father? Maybe there was a father or mother in the home, but he was not the ideal image of a father or she as a mother. Maybe it is not a prodigal son but a prodigal daughter. Maybe the person had good parents and a good home and through peer pressure or simple rebellion decided to go their own way, throw caution to the wind, and indulge in riotous living. Does any of this sound familiar?

So many times, we hear of children who end up on drugs or alcohol. It may be innocent at first, just partying with friends or a night out in town. Then they are destined to repeat the cycle of getting clean and then returning to the substance the first time they are stressed or are feeling inadequate or weak. The parents usually suffer through this and are drawn in by enabling behavior in hopes that their child will change. Searching for something to fill the loneliness or emptiness in their lives that they are feeling, they continue in this cycle until they hit rock bottom or something causes them to seek help for the addiction. So many lives are cut short, and so many lives are destroyed as a result. Maybe they think, *I am only hurting myself.* The reality is that they are hurting themselves and everyone in their lives and future generations with this behavior, in and out of jail, in and out of their parents' or grandparents' lives until they have no one to turn to or no one else to manipulate. Then they return home like the prodigal son.

In America, 142 people, on average, die from a drug overdose every day. Everywhere you look—on the news, in social media—headlines announce the latest scandals of pill mills, doctors overprescribing pain medications. You hear stories of parents overdosing with their children in the car. Even veterinarians are having to monitor pet owners for abuse of pain medication.

The CDC names three main types of opioids currently in use in the United States: prescription opioid painkillers (such as hydrocodone and OxyContin), fentanyl, and heroin. Fentanyl is a powerful synthetic opioid: it's up to one hundred times more powerful than morphine. Frighteningly, now emerging are super strong variations, like carfentanil, a lab-created elephant tranquilizer one hundred times more powerful than fentanyl.

It's true that America has one of the lowest alcohol use rates per capita, of first-world countries, with Belgium, Germany, France, the UK, and Australia coming out ahead of us. But we have a higher rate of alcohol abuse than any of those countries. About fifteen million American adults struggle with an alcohol use disorder.

In American culture, alcohol is used for celebration and commiseration alike. It has a sort of therapeutic role in our society. How often have you said after a long day or a stressful situation, "I need a drink"? Too often, we use alcohol, in general, and drunkenness, in particular, as a coping mechanism.

This unhealthy relationship gets imparted to us from a young age. College kids are notorious binge drinkers, and this is a culture adults help to perpetuate, accepting that college kids drink heavily. For many, alcohol has been taboo up to that point, so when they go away to college and get their hands on it for the first time, they don't understand how to moderate.

Ironically enough, all substance abuse programs—whether AA, NA, or counseling—have the person who's addicted rely on a higher power. Yes, God is the most important factor for a recovering addict. The other part of the equation is that you need to realize that you have a problem and admit that you need help. Only then can you begin the path to recovery. It is also important for the person to have a support system around them to help them get through the transition to recovery. I taught a Bible study in the jail and prison system mainly due to a high recidivism rate (people returning back into the system). I asked the question, What would keep you from returning to the system in the future after you are released? I received a myriad of answers, usually not the right ones. Occasionally, someone would speak up and say, "You need to change the people, places, and things in your life." That is the right answer.

The addicted person is usually in and out of relationships and clinging to people they think they love or people they think love them, usually just to have a place to stay. Most of the time, the relationship is superficial, and each person is manipulating the other for a lack of any other healthy relationship in their life. It can be very difficult to have a healthy relationship after this due to all the issues and emotional pain caused by the unhealthy relationships. They keep going back to their old friends, who are not real friends at all, to support their habit. They keep going back to the party lifestyle and the places that make them feel good. They are seeking a fulfillment that never comes. Then they need more of the substance to retain the same high or more superficial relationships to make them feel loved. The cycle continues on a downward spiral until they have no money, people are tired of their manipulation, and they have nowhere else to turn. There is a way out; however, it may not be easy to break a lifetime of wrong living. It takes God's help and a support system and a change of mind and heart.

When we fall into destructive behavior, we seek individuals who will be accepting of the behavior and to reassure us that we are okay, whether we are or not. The enabling person is just as destructive to the person as the addict themselves. One of the members of our church asked if she could speak with me after the service one Sunday. I assured her that I would make the time to have a conversation with her. She was a much-respected member of our community, a leader in our church, and read the Bible every day. She asked me if it were okay for her to pay her son's electric bill. She had made up her mind that it was fine, and she apparently wanted my approval. I knew her son very well and knew he struggled with a severe drug addiction. I asked her why she was paying for her son's drugs. She immediately got offended and said, "I am not paying for his drugs." I told her that she was being manipulated and that her son had spent the light bill money on drugs and that he was making her feel guilty because he would have two young sons in the dark if she did not pay the bill. She said, "You are right. I am supporting his habit, and he is manipulating me to get money to support this habit." She stopped paying his bills, and he eventually got off the drugs. He dedicated his life to Christ and became a different person. He reconciled with his family and enjoyed the remainder of his short life. He developed stage 4 lung cancer from smoking crack cocaine. Preaching at the funeral of one of my dearest friends was one of the hardest days of my life.

Having too little

It is more devastating when children are born into situations of crime, poverty, drugs, and neglect. Many times, they grow up in poverty in a single-parent home, and the mother has little education, and the state welfare system has to provide for the family. Thank God that we have the help from these programs. The church sometimes seems to have little involvement in helping people out of poverty. Many times, these young mothers and their families live in a run-down housing project in a neighborhood riddled with crime and drugs. Then the children grow up and repeat the same cycle as their parents. Research suggests that the characteristics of one's place of residence have important implications for the child and adult outcomes and that the negative consequences of childhood exposure to violence and drug dealing in areas of concentrated urban poverty may be particularly severe.

In many cases, the young mother cannot get a high enough paying job to get out of poverty and break this cycle. Single mothers and their children who live in substandard housing and in impoverished urban neighborhoods aspire for a better life but face overwhelming obstacles to achieving it. Sometimes, a close relative or grandparent will take the child in out of love. Although it is never really the ideal situation, some grandparents find that they need to raise their grandchildren because the parents of those children are not in a position to do so. Sometimes, it is because of financial circumstances, and sometimes, it is because of unsafe circumstances in the parent's home because of drug abuse. Whatever the case may be, more grandparents than ever before are stepping up to the plate in these situations. In these cases, the children are usually very fortunate.

Through social programs, church outreach programs, and educational opportunities, with encouragement and training, we have seen many lives changed. Some completed their education and went on to have rewarding careers. Some were able to become entrepreneurs. And some even continued to mentor others to change the trajectory of their lives. Poor families and urban mothers have many challenges in negotiating the many demands of parenting. Religion can serve as a resource in several ways. Resources associated with a church or faith-based organization, such as pastors, networks of fellow congregants, and material aid, can help change lives.

Having too much

Some children are spoiled and are given everything to compensate for the parents that are too busy to spend time with them or they are trying to compensate and make up for what they did not have as a child. Many times, children are not taught to manage their finances and fall into a pattern of having to be constantly bailed out by friends and family. I have a friend who is somewhat wealthy, and his daughter and son-in-law, two young professionals who both made good money, were constantly asking him to bail them out. He asked me for advice. I did not personally counsel them but advised they seek financial counseling, live within their means, and stop asking for a handout to pay for things they could not afford. They heeded the advice and finally got their lives on a solid financial footing.

It is not easy for a parent, a spouse, or a friend to release the person and encourage them to get help. Many times, the parent is contributing to the underlying emotional condition causing the pain. The Bible says to train up a child in the way they should go, and they will not depart from it when they are old. God is advising us to use biblical principles to raise our children. What God is saying here is that if we raise our children according to biblical principles, they may depart from it for a while, but they will return, much like the prodigal son, to a foundation of faith. Here comes the hard part: it is not easy when your child has gone astray to have faith that they will return. It is even harder to allow them to fail and have faith that they will have the strength to pick themselves back up again. Knowing when to intervene and when to take your hands off can be a very difficult decision.

We are definitely living in the me generation where everything has to benefit me. This is not a biblical principle. The Bible says to give, and it will be given back to you. We have a hard time sometimes in sacrificing our time and resources to make sure that our children learn the Scriptures and are taught about giving and loving others unconditionally. This is what the father did in the story of the prodigal son. He allowed his son to go out and live a party lifestyle; he allowed him to fail and allowed him to realize that he needed to take responsibility for his own decisions. He did not force his son to return to his previous lifestyle or make him come home. He waited until his son was ready to come home and opened his loving arms to him as he returned. He then let him know that he was a member of the family again. This is a story of our heavenly father and how he is willing to embrace us and take care of us when we are ready to return home. We do this by asking God and the people we have hurt for forgiveness, and restoration comes as a result.

On the other hand, the older brother in the story had an even bigger problem. He was self-righteous and did not feel that his brother deserved a second chance. So many times I see people who go to church, and God completely changes their life, and they become successful. Or they work hard to rise above poverty, and they become financially stable and then forget what God has blessed them with. They refuse to reach out to the lost and hurting and help pull them up by the hand when they are in need. Many times, we believe that we are helping others when in reality we are pushing them away by trying to make them into the person we want them to be. Instead, we need to allow them to be the person God created them to be.

We need more Christians to teach about finances, about family, and about family planning. The Bible says that God will provide us with everything we need and that we have everything that he has to offer and that we need to share it with those in need. If we believe that God has given us eternal life and provides us with everything we need, why would we be afraid to share his love with the world? So the message here is that even Christians need to walk humbly with God because he is our provider and sustains our life. I believe there are many who attend church who think they are saved because they are good people but have never truly surrendered their heart and life to Christ. The simple truth is that we can reach out to the lost and hurting and help the lost recover with the help of a loving God. More importantly, we can come together and solve many of these problems.

At the end of the story, the father ran toward his son to embrace him, demonstrating his unconditional love. He then celebrated the return of his son. He put on a great feast and lavished him with the finest clothes and jewelry. God is demonstrating to us that he wants us to have his very best. He is also demonstrating that we should not be envious of people who are blessed and restored. We should be grateful with what God has blessed us with. We should be equally grateful when God blesses someone else.

Jesus said, "Here I am! I stand at the door and knock. If anyone hears my voice and opens the door, I will come in and eat with that person, and they with me." It's quite a picture, isn't it? The God of the universe, word become flesh, Jesus himself, standing humbly and patiently at the door to someone's house, knocking gently. These are the words we read in Revelation 3:20, "Here I am! I stand at the door and knock. If anyone hears my voice and opens the door, I will come in and eat with that person, and they with me." Jesus seeks to save those who are lost; he also wants to reach out to believers who are off track and bring them closer to God.

THE BLIND MAN

According to the Gospel of John 9:1–12, Jesus saw a man who had been blind since birth. His disciples asked him, "Rabbi, who sinned, this man or his parents, that he was born blind?"

This is a story of a man who was blind from birth. Jesus miraculously healed the man and sent him on his way. The story does not end there. It was customary for a person who was healed to go to the temple and show themselves to the priest. The leaders of the temple questioned the young man and his parents. Because the leaders could not deny the miracle, they began to question the authority and power of Jesus. They wanted the young man to say that Jesus did not perform the miracle. The young man refused to deny it and was expelled from the temple. To be expelled from the temple meant that he and his parents would have been shunned from society.

Jesus is showing us that he can heal physical ailments and restore lives and families. At the same time, he is teaching that many times, spiritual leaders are blind themselves to the needs of people and blind to what God is able to do. This is a story of God wanting to heal us and bring us to a true knowledge of his loving kindness and his ability to direct our focus.

When questioned about why the man was blind, Jesus addressed the disciples by saying, "Neither this man nor his parents sinned…but this happened so that the works of God might be displayed in him. As long as it is day, we must do the works of him who sent me. Night is coming, when no one can work. While I am in the world, I am the light of the world. God is intending here to show that true light and reflection into the heart of man can only come from him."

Having said this, Jesus spat on the ground and anointed the man's eyes with a mixture of mud and saliva. He told the blind man to go and wash in the Pool of Siloam; the Bible narrative adds that the word "Siloam" means "sent." The man "went and washed and came home seeing." God is showing us here that indeed he created the world and that he created man from the dust of the ground, as described in the Scriptures. He then recreated the man's eyes from the same dust.

When they saw him, those who had known him as a blind beggar asked if this was the same man. Some said that he was while others said, "No, he only looks like him."

But the man himself said, "I am the man" (Greek: *egō eimi*, literally: "I am"). When we witness a miracle, we tend to seek out a logical, scientific explanation.

The remainder of the chapter relates the investigation of the miracle by the Pharisees. Jesus makes use of the occasion to deliver a metaphorical teaching that he came into the world "so that the blind may see."

Let's examine the Scriptures in John 9:1–41.

Jesus Heals a Man Born Blind

As he went along, he saw a man blind from birth. His disciples asked him, "Rabbi, who sinned, this man or his parents, that he was born blind?"

"Neither this man nor his parents sinned," said Jesus, "but this happened so that the works of God might be displayed in him. As long as it is day, we must do the works of him who sent me. Night is coming, when no one can work. While I am in the world, I am the light of the world."

After saying this, he spit on the ground, made some mud with the saliva, and put it on the man's eyes. "Go," he told him, "wash in the Pool of Siloam" (this word means "Sent"). So the man went and washed, and came home seeing.

His neighbors and those who had formerly seen him begging asked, "Isn't this the same man who used to sit and beg?" Some claimed that he was.

Others said, "No, he only looks like him."

But he himself insisted, "I am the man."

"How then were your eyes opened?" they asked.

He replied, "The man they call Jesus made some mud and put it on my eyes. He told me to go to Siloam and wash. So I went and washed, and then I could see."

"Where is this man?" they asked him.

"I don't know," he said.

The Pharisees Investigate the Healing

They brought to the Pharisees the man who had been blind. Now the day on which Jesus had made the mud and opened the man's eyes was a Sabbath. Therefore, the Pharisees also asked him how he had received his sight. "He put mud on my eyes," the man replied, "and I washed, and now I see."

Some of the Pharisees said, "This man is not from God, for he does not keep the Sabbath."

But others asked, "How can a sinner perform such signs?" So they were divided.

Then they turned again to the blind man, "What have you to say about him? It was your eyes he opened."

The man replied, "He is a prophet."

They still did not believe that he had been blind and had received his sight until they sent for the man's parents. "Is this your son?" they asked. "Is this the one you say was born blind? How is it that now he can see?"

"We know he is our son," the parents answered, "and we know he was born blind. But how he can see now, or who opened his eyes, we don't know. Ask him. He is of age; he will speak for himself." His parents said this because they were afraid of the Jewish leaders, who already had decided that anyone who acknowledged that Jesus was the Messiah would be put out of the synagogue. That was why his parents said, "He is of age; ask him."

A second time they summoned the man who had been blind. "Give glory to God by telling the truth," they said. "We know this man is a sinner."

He replied, "Whether he is a sinner or not, I don't know. One thing I do know. I was blind but now I see!"

Then they asked him, "What did he do to you? How did he open your eyes?"

He answered, "I have told you already and you did not listen. Why do you want to hear it again? Do you want to become his disciples too?"

Then they hurled insults at him and said, "You are this fellow's disciple! We are disciples of Moses! We know that God spoke to Moses, but as for this fellow, we don't even know where he comes from."

The man answered, "Now that is remarkable! You don't know where he comes from, yet he opened my eyes. We know that God does not listen to sinners. He listens to the godly person who does his will. Nobody has ever heard of opening the eyes of a man born blind. If this man were not from God, he could do nothing."

To this they replied, "You were steeped in sin at birth; how dare you lecture us!" And they threw him out.

Spiritual Blindness

Jesus heard that they had thrown him out, and when he found him, he said, "Do you believe in the Son of Man?"

"Who is he, sir?" the man asked. "Tell me so that I may believe in him."

Jesus said, "You have now seen him; in fact, he is the one speaking with you."

Then the man said, "Lord, I believe," and he worshiped him.

Jesus said, "For judgment I have come into this world, so that the blind will see and those who see will become blind."

Some Pharisees who were with him heard him say this and asked, "What? Are we blind too?"

Jesus said, "If you were blind, you would not be guilty of sin; but now that you claim you can see, your guilt remains.

Let's examine the story of the man born blind.

The disciples asked Jesus, "Who sinned? This blind man or his parents?"

Jesus replied, "Neither one sinned, but that the works of God would be revealed in him." Jesus then made mud with dirt and his spit and placed it on the man's eyes and told him to go to the Pool of Siloam and wash it off.

The Bible says that he came back with his sight. What a miracle, not only did he open the eyes of a blind man but he also figuratively opened the eyes of all who knew the man. He also opened the eyes of the religious leadership. The people had heard that God had performed miracles in the past and had moved in many ways to show forth his power. Who was this man Jesus who could take a man blind from birth and literally recreate his eyes from the very soil from which he was formed?

Have you ever seen someone on the side of the road or at an intersection begging for change? This was the plight of the blind man. He could not work for a living. They did not have the disabilities act then to help the young man. The person was considered an outcast. They blamed it on sin when in reality, he had a disability from birth. The only way the man could earn a living was to beg for money. I am sure his parents lived with constant guilt and shame. The religious leaders thought that all illness was brought on by some type of sin, either in the person or their parents. So for him to receive his sight was a marvelous thing; for the family to receive their standing in the community again was equally as wonderful. What a transformation in his life and the life of his family.

The blind man did as Jesus asked him to do, and he was healed. What a way for God to display his power. This man was blind all his life; the whole community knew him and knew his parents. There was no way they could deny what had happened. They could, however, try to explain it away. What was Jesus trying to accomplish? Were the leaders trying to hold on to power at all cost, even at the expense of a blind man and his family? Jesus was showing the leaders that he was God and that he made the rules and not them. He displayed to the world that day that he was the Son of God. But rather than being happy for the man who was healed, the leaders hurled insults at the man and at God.

Have you ever needed healing or needed help with food or rent and were ashamed to ask for help? Maybe you do not need physical healing; maybe you need an emotional or psychological healing or possibly, like the people in this story, you need a spiritual healing. Ask God for help in prayer; you may be surprised that he answers your prayers. He is an all-powerful, wonderful, loving God, and yes, he does still heal people and restores families today.

Sometimes, we pray, and he does not heal us or answer us right away, and we doubt that he will. Maybe he will just give you strength to get you through the pain. The Bible says to wait on the Lord, and he will renew your strength. The blind man had waited from the time he was born until he was grown to receive his sight. The Bible also says that God does not see as we see. Man looks on the outward appearance, but God examines the heart. In other words, if the spiritual condition is right, then all the external things that we think are important really do not matter as much. If we have that kind of insight, we can see the things that are important in life and live a life that is pleasing to God.

The religious leaders were angry that Jesus healed the blind man. Who does he think he is opening the blind man's eyes and on the Sabbath? Really, God performs a miracle like this, and all they can think of to discredit it is that it was done on the wrong day. Well, I'm sure the blind man could care less what day it was. He said, "All I know is that I was blind, and now I see." As a matter of fact, he was so grateful he became a follower of Jesus, so much so that he tried to convince the religious leaders to follow Jesus. Are you a follower of Jesus? Does he need to open your eyes?

After they tested the young man to see how he was healed, they summoned his parents to confirm that this was their son. They testified before the Jewish leaders and confirmed that indeed this was their son and that he was born blind. They were afraid to say that Jesus healed him because the leaders declared that anyone who followed Jesus would be expelled from the temple. In those days, in this society, if you were kicked out of the temple, you were shunned by society. What a shame, God heals their son, and they are unable to proclaim it. Out of fear, they told the leaders to ask their son who healed him because he was a grown man. Keep in mind this is legal testimony as if you were in court today.

They summoned the young man to testify again. They tried to get him to recant his testimony by accusing Jesus of being a sinner; they hurled insults at the young man and continued to threaten him. The young man refused to change his story and was kicked out of the temple. He forsook the only religion he ever knew because he knew that he had been healed by God. He embraced Christ and the new message he was teaching. Imagine being completely blind all your life and suddenly you received your sight. Would you believe in Jesus Christ? Amazingly enough, the religious leaders saw the miracle and yet refused to believe.

Jesus saw the young man shortly after he was expelled from the temple. Jesus asked the young man, "Do you believe in the Son of Man?"

The young man replied, "Who is the Son of Man that I may believe in him?"

Jesus then replied, "You are looking at him."

Imagine being healed by God, then looking at the Son of God directly.

The Bible says that the young man believed, called Jesus Lord, and worshipped him. The young man accepted Christ as the result of a healing. Do you need God to bring a healing in your life? Why was God so concerned with this man who would seem so insignificant to us?

Jesus said, "For judgment I have come into this world, so that the blind will see and those who see will become blind." The teachers and leaders asked Jesus if they were blind. Jesus replied that they were indeed blind, and as a result, they would not be saved. He went on to explain that if they had not been spiritually blind, they might receive eternal life. Because they were so stubborn in their religious tradition and refused the signs of the Messiah that they had read in the Scriptures, they were essentially expelled from the kingdom of God just like they did to the young man. Will you go on into eternity with God?

Jesus tells us that he is the Messiah and that the only way to see God is through salvation in him. The Scriptures say Jesus asked the man if he knew who he was.

The man healed of blindness responded, "Tell me so that I may believe in him."

Jesus said, "You have now seen him; in fact, he is the one speaking with you. For judgment I have come into this world, so that the blind will see and those who see will become blind."

The reference here to those who see versus those who are blind is meant to explain this entire incident with the blind beggar and the religious critics. Those who admit their need and trust in God are those who will be granted sight. The blind man was given both sight and knowledge of salvation by Jesus in response to his sincere faith. Those who are arrogant and presume they already know everything will be hardened by the presence of Jesus instead. Despite their knowledge, they'll allow their own prejudice to blind them, making them incapable of understanding what God wants them to see.

THE WOMAN WITH THE ISSUE OF BLOOD

This story is about a woman who spent all her resources on physicians because she had an incurable disease. Because of the continual bleeding, the woman would have been continually regarded in Jewish law as a niddah or menstruating woman and so ceremonially unclean. To be regarded as clean, the flow of blood would need to stop for at least seven days. Because of the constant bleeding, this woman lived in a continual state of uncleanness, which would have brought upon her social and religious isolation. It would have prevented her from getting married or if she was already married when the bleeding started, she would have prevented her from having sexual relations with her husband and might have been cited by him as grounds for divorce.

The unnamed woman in this Gospel story was a woman who had suffered for twelve years from a certain kind of bleeding; it was often translated as "hemorrhaging." She had visited many doctors and healers, and none of them had been able to heal her. It seemed frenetic and like she was acting out in a last-ditch effort. Her very presence in a large crowd would be frowned upon in this society because she was considered "unclean." Her normal existence would often have been spent watching people skirt around her to avoid the possibility of contact. No brushing or touching or sharing friendly gestures on the path. She lived in isolation and would have been known for her uncleanliness. This is a story of hope when there seems to be no hope and help where there seems to be no help.

Let's read the Scriptures in Mark 5:25–34.

> And a woman was there who had been subject to bleeding for twelve years. She had suffered a great deal under the care of many doctors and had spent all she had, yet instead of getting better she grew worse. When she heard about Jesus, she came up behind him in the crowd and touched his cloak, because she thought, "If I just touch his clothes, I will be healed." Immediately her bleeding stopped and she felt in her body that she was freed from her suffering.
>
> At once Jesus realized that power had gone out from him. He turned around in the crowd and asked, "Who touched my clothes?"
>
> "You see the people crowding against you," his disciples answered, "and yet you can ask, 'Who touched me?'"
>
> But Jesus kept looking around to see who had done it. Then the woman, knowing what had happened to her, came and

fell at his feet and, trembling with fear, told him the whole truth. He said to her, "Daughter, your faith has healed you. Go in peace and be freed from your suffering.

Let's examine the story a little closer

The woman, the Bible says, spent all her resources on doctors, and no one could heal her. The woman was getting worse medically, most likely to the point of death. She heard that Jesus was in town and heard of the miracles he performed. She thought, *If I can just touch him, I will be healed.* After she touched his garment, she was afraid when Jesus turned around and realized what had happened. Most likely, the fear came from the fact that she was instructed by the religious leaders and doctors not to come in close contact with anyone. They were afraid someone else would become ill as a result.

When she reached out to be healed, Jesus looked at her and said, "Go your way. Your faith has made you well." In the large crowd following Jesus and others getting healed, the woman, through faith, reached out in hopes that she would be healed. The great faith of the woman touched the heart of God, and he noticed the woman that society and the medical community had given up on. Even in the chaos of the crowd, God recognized the needs of a single person who was seeking after him. The Bible says that his eye is on the sparrow, meaning, the smallest of things. If we bring even the small things to God in faith, he will answer our prayers.

Imagine that kind of faith and the impact it would have on the world today—in a world where people are ashamed to share their faith in fear of what someone might think. In retrospect, the woman was glad that she made the choice to believe in Christ and believe that he could heal her. Imagine her waking up the next morning free from pain and suffering. Imagine the look on the doctor's face when she returned for an examination and she was completely healed. We need that kind of faith today. That is the kind of faith that says, "I don't care what society thinks. I need a touch from God, and I am going to press in until I receive it."

In our time, having lived through a global pandemic, I see it as a sign of the things to come on the earth, having to wear a mask and afraid of everyone around you. Millions of people are dying around the world. The news stations are reporting freezers filled with the dead in large cities. In a time we call modern medicine and all the scientific breakthroughs, we still do not have all the answers. We need to reach out to God in these trying times in prayer and trust that he is able to help solve a global crisis. It is good to follow the best medical advice of the time; however, medical technology is always advancing and does not always have the answers. Like the woman in this story, there is not always a medical cure. Only when she had exhausted all her resources did she finally turn to God for answers.

The impact of a medical crisis on the world today

The year 2020 will go down as one of the most turbulent times in human history. The COVID-19 pandemic has not only impacted the world but it also has particularly impacted the minority and poor communities. The cost is upward of 10 percent of the world's income. More than seventy million people came into extreme poverty as a result, and the number is rising. Around 1.6 million students were out of school. People were unemployed in certain industries. Entire cities and nations were on lockdown. Only essential workers were required to report to work to keep the economy moving.

Family members were isolated in nursing homes and hospitals. Others were unable to visit relatives or even spend the holidays together. Medical staff was just as vulnerable as the general population. I had friends who were unable to visit their loved ones as they lay dying. I preached at a funeral for a dear friend during the peak of the pandemic. Most people were avoiding even having a funeral service for their loved ones. The service was held outdoors, and people sat in their cars to hear the eulogy.

Churches were closed, and the ones that remained open were controlled by the government. No more than fifty people in a crowd and then no more than ten. Church services were then streamed online, and meetings were held via video instead of in-person meetings. The government took complete control of our lives. There were mandates to wear a mask in public. Then the vaccines were produced and mandated by business and government. People were fired for not submitting to the mandates. Businesses were closed due to a lack of staffing and fear. Restaurants had restrictions on the number of patrons or were closed due to government restrictions.

During this time, large scale riots, looting, and anarchy broke out in American cities in the name of social justice. People were being killed in retribution for police killings. Public buildings were set on fire, the blaze filmed and displayed on national television for the entire world to see. Fire departments and law enforcement and first responders were unable to enter the hot zones to assist. A literal war had broken out in protest across a nation, and in some cities, the government officials encouraged the violence. The church largely stood in silence as political factions used inflammatory rhetoric to move their agenda forward.

Tracking citizens and government control

Global tracking devices otherwise known as cell phones are used to track people around the world. A national alert system was set up and sent to all cell phone users by the federal government in case of a national emergency. A surveillance system was set up after America was attacked on September 11, 2001, called the Patriot Act. This system was designed to spy on terrorists communicating with terrorist networks. Then it was used to track ordinary citizens. Now the federal government is setting up a truth commission similar to the communication controls in place in communist China.

The US Centers for Disease Control and Prevention tracked millions of Americans' phones to see if they complied with lockdowns and vaccination efforts during the COVID-19 pandemic. The federal agency used location data from cell phones to monitor visits to churches and schools, as well as to pharmacies for "vaccine monitoring." The data also showed movement during curfews and visits between neighbors when people were encouraged to stay home, practice social distancing, and avoid social gatherings. The CDC has "extremely accurate insights related to age, gender, race, citizenship status, income, and more" based on the data. The CDC said it wants to continue using the information for more than pandemic monitoring, such as tracking "population migration before, during, and after natural disasters" and researching visits to parks and gyms for interest in exercise and chronic disease prevention.

The Scripture states, concerning the Antichrist, if one has understanding to count the number of the beast, which is also the number of a man, and his number is six hundred threescore and six. Each person has a tracking code from the government on our phone to track for our every move. People are censored and banned from social media sites for simply expressing their faith. This is the beginning of the mark of the beast mentioned in the Bible in the book of Revelations. The mark referred to is put on the forehead of those who worship the beast, the Antichrist and symbol of opposition to God. Could this simply mean that people are mentally opposed to God and will work diligently to undermine the teachings of Christ and the Bible in the last days? Could this simply mean a device held in your hand while examined by your eyes and taken into your mind?

God is voted out of society

In our educational system that is funded by the government and controlled by the teachers' union, God has been voted out of school. The same educational system is teaching students to hate one another based on their cultural, religious, social, racial, and sexual identity. The court ruled that under the establishment clause of the First Amendment, "it is no part of the business of government to compose official prayers for any group of the American people to recite as a part of a religious program carried on by government." In other words, state-sponsored prayers in schools are unconstitutional. Students, on the other hand, are fully free to pray in public schools, alone or in groups, as long as they don't disrupt the school or interfere with the rights of others.

Prayer has not been taken out of schools or government. The First Amendment of our constitution guarantees the right to pray and speak about your faith. The law simply states that the government cannot make you participate in religious activities. The educational system is indoctrinating students to make them believe they have no right to have faith. As a matter of fact, religious accommodation laws were passed to guarantee you the freedom to pray and practice your faith without interference from an educator or the government.

Why the church is needed more today

How does faith affect society? Christianity promotes the well-being of individuals, families, and communities. Religious worship also leads to a reduction in the incidence of domestic abuse, crime, substance abuse, and addiction. In addition, religious practice can increase physical and mental health, longevity, and educational attainment.

Christ tells us to love people for who they are

Have you ever had a hard time "fitting in" somewhere? Whether it be at school or work, in a new group of friends, or even your own family, we can all relate to feeling unaccepted at one time or another. On the other hand, many of us can think of a time that we had trouble accepting someone else. It is important that the church accept people for who they are and makes them feel welcome.

Acceptance is the ability to see that others have a right to be their own unique persons. That means having a right to their own feelings, thoughts, and opinions. When you accept people for who they are, you let go of your desire to change them. You let them feel the way they want to feel; you let them be different and think differently from you. Everyone is different in one way or another. Once you understand this truth, you can stop trying to change them into the people you want them to be and start accepting them for who they are.

Acceptance of others' feelings is not easy when people act differently than we do. We all have trouble accepting those who are different. By learning the skill of empathy, we will be better able to understand ourselves and those who are different from us.

Freedom to speak the truth

Freedom of speech and the First Amendment protect everyone, religious and nonreligious alike, from the government becoming so powerful that it can tell people what to think and how to act. Conscience has been considered the individual's most sacred right. A government that intrudes on conscience will not hesitate to intrude on our other freedoms. The Bible says that in the last days, people will be persecuted for having faith and believing that all our rights come from God. Will you continue to have faith if you are attacked for believing in God? Will you continue to have faith if your biblical values conflict with medical, political, and social mandates? Is God being expelled from our churches like Jesus was kicked out of the temple in favor of a more contemporary religion meant to attract religious observers rather than transform lives? The Bible says to speak the truth in love. Without a spiritual guidepost, we have no clear direction in life.

As the political divide grows deeper in our country, the way we're relating with those we disagree with is deteriorating. It's always challenging to show kindness to those we disagree with, but today it almost seems unthinkable. How do we handle conflicting relationships? Do we end the relationship with people we disagree with? Is it possible to accept or continue to accept someone who disagrees with us theologically, politically, or socially? The answer is to be who you are and allow people to accept you for just that.

The kind of "accept" I'm referring to is welcoming them, embracing them, and adopting them as they are regardless of what they have. The Bible says for us to come to God just the way we are.

> My brothers, show no partiality as you hold the faith in our Lord Jesus Christ, the Lord of glory. For if a man wearing a gold ring and fine clothing comes into your assembly, and a poor man in shabby clothing also comes in, and if you pay attention to the one who wears the fine clothing and say, "You sit here in a good place," while you say to the poor man, "You stand over there," or, "Sit down at my feet," have you not then made distinctions among yourselves and become judges with evil thoughts? Listen, my beloved brothers, has not God chosen those who are poor in the world to be rich in faith and heirs of the kingdom, which he has promised to those who love him? (James 2: 1–26)

If you are living for Christ, you can impact their lives in a positive way. Accepting someone means you love them today, just as they are, with all their victories and failures. There's plenty of biblical support for this position.

Jesus talks about such love in Matthew 5:46, "If you love only those who love you, what reward is there for that?" Jesus also reminds us to imitate God's posture toward others in Luke 6:35–36, "For he [God] is kind to those who are unthankful and wicked. You must be compassionate, just as your Father is compassionate." Several years later in Romans 2:4, Paul asked Roman Christians to reflect God's example in loving those who make life choices that lead to sin, "Don't you see how wonderfully kind, tolerant, and patient God is with you? Does this mean nothing to you? Can't you see that his kindness is intended to turn you from your sin?"

I can't help but wonder if God's kindness leads people to repentance; won't my kindness lead people to God? Later in the same book, Paul says, "Do all that you can to live in peace with everyone" (Romans 12:18). The author of Hebrews reminds us of the importance of being loving toward people we don't even know.

CATCHING A FISH WITH A COIN IN ITS MOUTH

Jesus was tested by the religious leaders of his day to pay taxes. The temple tax was also mentioned in the New Testament in Matthew 17:24–27 when Peter was confronted by the religious leaders collecting the tax. The leaders asked Peter, "Doesn't your teacher pay the temple tax?" The leaders might have been attempting to prove Jesus' disloyalty to the temple or his violation of the law. Peter affirmed that Jesus did pay the temple tax. When Peter came into the house where Jesus was, the Lord asked him, "From whom do the kings of the earth collect duty and taxes—from their own children or from others?" Peter replied that kings collected from others because their children were exempt. Jesus' point was that since the temple was his father's house, Jesus was exempt.

Even though Jesus, as the Son of God, and his disciples were exempt from paying the temple tax, they would pay the tax to not offend the Jewish leaders (Matthew 17:27). Jesus then instructed Peter to throw out a fishing line, which would result in a catch. When Peter opened the fish's mouth, he found a coin that happened to be the correct amount for the temple tax for him and Jesus.

Jesus used the question about the temple tax to teach a lesson. Christians are free, but they must sometimes relinquish their rights to uphold their witness and not cause others to stumble. True freedom is not serving our self but serving others. This is a story of God's provision for us in times of need.

Let's review the Scriptures in Matthew 17:24–27.

The Temple Tax

After Jesus and his disciples arrived in Capernaum, the collectors of the two-drachma temple tax came to Peter and asked, "Doesn't your teacher pay the temple tax?"

"Yes, he does," he replied.

When Peter came into the house, Jesus was the first to speak. "What do you think, Simon?" he asked. "From whom do the kings of the earth collect duty and taxes—from their own children or from others?"

"From others," Peter answered.

"Then the children are exempt," Jesus said to him. "But so that we may not cause offense, go to the lake and throw out your line. Take the first fish you catch; open its mouth and you will find a four-drachma coin. Take it and give it to them for my tax and yours."

Let's review this story.

Peter was questioned by the community leaders if Jesus was required to pay taxes. Peter was a professional fisherman by trade. He would have paid taxes on a regular basis. The temple at the time was the center of the government, and the taxes were required for upkeep of the temple. The taxes were intended for a certain use; however, over time, legislation was passed to use the money for other than the original intention. That sounds a lot like our government and even some of our churches today.

Peter asked Jesus if they were required to pay the taxes. Jesus explained to Peter that he was indeed exempt from paying taxes because he was the Son of God. Jesus told Peter that they would pay the tax because it was the way to set an example to society.

Jesus then told Peter to go out and cast a fishing line in the water and that he would catch a fish with a coin in its mouth. Peter did not doubt Jesus and did as Jesus asked. Peter caught a fish with a coin in the exact amount as the tax owed by him and Jesus. Peter then paid the tax.

Peter was an outspoken man who tended to act before he thought. He was one of the first disciples of Christ and was chosen by God as one of the leaders of the church. God was teaching him that we were to submit to government authority whether we agreed with the rules or not.

Taxes today

Around the world, taxes are paid for education, national security, and government programs. This is a necessary part of keeping a society functioning properly. Many times, however, money is wasted on a political or social cause that does not benefit the society. Jesus truly cared for the poor and the hurting and commanded us to take care of them. If you understand the New Testament Scriptures, it compels us to love one another as much as God loves us. If the church and Christians came together with that kind of love, what a different world this would be.

The Bible clearly states that there is to be no division in the church. Jesus was speaking directly to the religious leaders of his day to stop trying to hold on to power and help the helpless as the Scriptures required. To take taxes from the masses to social engineer a society was not what Jesus was teaching; it was just the opposite. He preached directly to the ones whom society looked down upon and to those in need. He lifted up the hurting and poor and elevated them to the same status as the highest members of society. Jesus was mocked for hanging out with people who were considered sinners. His friends were just like us, down-to-earth, ordinary people with ordinary problems that needed to be solved.

Taxation and what it is used for today

We should be thankful for the medical and scientific advancements that have been made in recent history. In the middle of a global pandemic, scientists were able to quickly find a vaccine to save lives. If this pandemic had struck in the past, the loss would be beyond belief. Some of the technology today is now being used for biomedical research, both good and bad. Doctors and scientists are experimenting with viruses, human biology, and cosmetic surgery in the name of benefitting humanity. The consequences will have a further impact than we could ever imagine.

As the government continues to reach into our pockets to benefit their current constituency and lobbyists, our nation and world are tearing apart at the seams. In our current society, there is pending legislation in America to give the government access to all bank accounts to review every transaction. Imagine the government raiding your business or church just to pay for more government programs. The excess spending is causing high inflation and the cost of all goods to go up in price. We are not only losing religious freedom around the world; we are losing the war on individual freedoms. The money spent fighting the pandemic is in the multiple trillions of dollars. There were almost seven trillion dollars spent so far, and the bills are climbing.

The result is that the cost of goods is going up astronomically. Food prices are up by 10 percent; fuel prices increase by one-third. Money is borrowed from foreign governments to pay for all the excessive spending. The national debt is over twenty-seven trillion dollars. How are our grandchildren going to pay for all this? New government entitlements are being added as I write this book. Social Security, Medicare, and Medicaid could be insolvent in a few years; however, we feel the need to add on to this climbing debt. Entire nations are struggling to maintain a global economic system. Can this be sustained? Will the system fail?

Taxes used for war

Prior to the global pandemic, America spent trillions of dollars fighting what seemed like endless wars. The war in Iraq and Afghanistan were fought to control terrorism. In reality, after almost twenty years of war, the threat from the terrorist still looms large. The Taliban, a terrorist organization, are now in control of Afghanistan. Iraq is not the Middle East democracy that the military had hoped for. The Middle East is still in chaos, and America and Israel are just as hated as they were before the wars. We seek to control other nations while we are neglecting education, health care, the elderly, poverty, and housing in our own nation. If we are truly following Christ, then we would come together across religious, political, and socioeconomic divides to solve the problems we are faced with in this country and around the world.

Where do we turn for relief? Where do we turn for answers?

The answer is in the Scriptures.

Second Chronicles 7:14 says, "If my people, which are called by my name, shall humble themselves, and pray, and seek my face, and turn from their wicked ways; then will I hear from heaven, and will forgive their sin, and will heal their land."

The Bible says that if we would repent and ask God for forgiveness and live by his principles, then he will restore our lives and the land. The church is afraid to speak out on many of these issues in fear of losing their tax-exempt status because legislation has been passed to call biblical teaching hate speech.

The Scriptures say that blessed are the merciful for they will be shown mercy. Mercy comes from a heart that has first felt its spiritual bankruptcy. The heart has come to grieve its sin and has learned to wait meekly for the timing of the Lord and to cry out in hunger for the work of God's mercy to satisfy us with the righteousness we need. To receive mercy from God, the Scriptures say that we are to show mercy to our fellow man. The most important laws of human conduct are religious in nature, things like mercy, forgiveness, neighborly care, hospitality, and love for one's enemies. Do we really have faith that God will hear from heaven and that he can heal our land?

JESUS FEEDS FIVE THOUSAND PEOPLE

The feeding of the five thousand is also known as the miracle of the five loaves and two fish; the Gospel of John reports that Jesus used five loaves and two fish supplied by a boy to feed a multitude. According to Matthew's Gospel, when Jesus heard that John the Baptist had been killed, he withdrew by boat privately to a solitary place. Luke specified that the place was near Bethsaida. The crowds followed Jesus on foot from the towns. When Jesus landed and saw a large crowd, he had compassion on them and healed their sick. As evening approached, the disciples came to him and said, "This is a remote place. It's already getting late. Send the crowds away, so they can go to the villages and buy themselves some food."

Jesus said that they did not need to go away, and therefore, the disciples were to give them something to eat. They said that they only had five loaves and two fish, which Jesus asked to be brought to him. Jesus directed the people to sit down in groups on the grass. In Mark's Gospel, the crowds sat in groups of fifty and one hundred; and in Luke's Gospel, Jesus's instructions were to seat the crowd in groups of fifty, implying that there were one hundred such groups.

Taking the five loaves and the two fish and looking up to heaven, he gave thanks and broke them. Then he gave them to the disciples, and the disciples gave them to the people. They all ate and were satisfied, and the disciples picked up twelve baskets full of broken pieces that were leftovers. The number of those who ate was about five thousand men, besides women and children.

In John's Gospel, the multitude had been attracted around Jesus because of the healing works he had performed, and the feeding of the multitude was taken as a further sign that Jesus was the Messiah. This is a story of God's desire to feed the hungry and to teach us that if we give to those who are hungry, he will multiply what we have.

Let's read the Scriptures in Matthew 14:13–21.

Jesus Feeds the Five Thousand

When Jesus heard what had happened, he withdrew by boat privately to a solitary place. Hearing of this, the crowds followed him on foot from the towns. When Jesus landed and saw a large crowd, he had compassion on them and healed their sick.

As evening approached, the disciples came to him and said, "This is a remote place, and it's already getting late. Send the crowds away, so they can go to the villages and buy themselves some food."

Jesus replied, "They do not need to go away. You give them something to eat."

"We have here only five loaves of bread and two fish," they answered.

"Bring them here to me," he said. And he directed the people to sit down on the grass. Taking the five loaves and the two fish and looking up to heaven, he gave thanks and broke the loaves. Then he gave them to the disciples, and the disciples gave them to the people. They all ate and were satisfied, and the disciples picked up twelve baskets full of broken pieces that were left over. The number of those who ate was about five thousand men, besides women and children.

Let's examine the Scriptures

Jesus had just been notified that John the Baptist was killed for preaching the Gospel. Not only was John the predecessor to Jesus and taught of his coming but also his mother, Elisabeth, was first cousins to Jesus's mother, Mary. The Scriptures say that Jesus was seeking to get away from the crowd to be alone. He took a boat to an isolated location.

The town of Bethsaida heard of this and followed Jesus to this isolated place. Most likely, Jesus was attempting to pray and possibly grieve. They followed him to the isolated location for his teaching and for healing. Jesus put his own needs aside and began to minister to the crowd. It started to get late in the evening, and the disciples approached Jesus to send the crowd away to get food. Jesus instructed the disciples not to send the crowd away and told them to provide food themselves. Can you imagine the look on his disciples' faces when he said for them to provide food and they realized that there was only enough for a few people?

The disciples responded to the request to provide food by saying that all they had was two fish and five loaves of bread. Jesus then instructed the crowd to be seated in groups of fifty and one hundred on the grass. Jesus then took the two fish and five loaves of bread and lifted it up to heaven; he prayed and thanked God for the provisions. He then instructed the disciples to distribute the food. They handed out food until every person had enough to eat and were satisfied. The leftovers filled twelve baskets full to the brim. The disciples learned that day that God could provide whatever they needed not only to sustain them but also enough to provide for five-thousand-plus people. God is teaching us that true provision comes from him and that he is the sustainer of life.

Hunger and Poverty in the World Today

Biblical values encourage Christians to take responsibility to help combat hunger and to help those in need. Christians are admonished in the Scriptures to feed the poor and take care of those in need. Climate change, government spending, wars, natural disasters, and a pandemic will strike hard against the very people we're told to care for and love, amplifying hunger and poverty and increasing

risks of resource scarcity that can exacerbate political insta-
bility and even create or worsen the refugee crises.

Those living in impoverished countries or locations
generally aren't physically or economically equipped to deal
with the changing environment or to rebuild after frequent
natural disasters often linked to climate change. In these
same places, health conditions are linked to lower air qual-
ity and rampant disease that their medical system is unable
to deal with.

Changes in the health care system have also contributed to the homeless crisis and crime in America. People
with medical and mental issues and substance abuse issues
are forced on the streets. The homeless represent the most
vulnerable portion of Americans living in poverty. The
latest US government report on homelessness shows that
a culture of secularism is depriving Americans of church
philanthropy, curbing the free market's ability to provide
and leaving the most vulnerable reliant on the government
or the mercy of the streets.

Millions of immigrants are flooding into America.
Efforts to end global poverty and to secure the most basic
human rights for the poor are failing because crime and
violence against the poor are not being addressed. Changes
to the institutionalization process have made it impossible
for people with severe mental illness to find appropriate
care and shelter, resulting in homelessness or "housing" in
the criminal justice system's jails and prisons.

In all countries, both developed and developing, older
people face an array of vulnerabilities. Among these are
lack of income, health insecurity, and the need for phys-

ical care. Most of us in the United States have incredibly fortunate lives compared to the rest of the world. While we have worked hard for what we have, we must recognize that there are many people in the world who have also worked hard without the same results. Indeed, we have benefited greatly from the collective acts of many who came before us. They have built a system and nation that have made our great lives possible. Each and every one of us is very lucky to be here.

There are many people in the rest of the world who are incredibly poor. Many starve to death. Many more are chronically hungry. Many men, women, and children have no opportunity to improve their lives. Currently, the United Nations estimates that nearly 385 million children around the world are living below the universal poverty line. They also have fewer options available to them to break the cycle of poverty given that they have fewer agencies than adults and are often the subjects of abuse and mistreatment as a direct result of poverty. The reality for them is that there is no economic opportunity, no system or nation in place for them to succeed. This plight of poverty is not their fault. It is simply a result of being born into the wrong circumstances.

The Bible teaches us to be thankful for what we have and to be happy. God tells us to pray and ask for what we need for our provision and enough to help provide for others. The Scriptures say, "Rejoice always, pray continually, and give thanks in all circumstances; for this is God's will for you in Christ Jesus." The good news: God wants you to be happy, to pray to him, and to always be thankful for all the blessings in your life. The Scriptures say, "Give thanks to the Lord, for he is good; his love endures forever."

When the Lord Returns

Jesus said, "When the Son of Man comes in his glory and all the angels with him, he will sit on his throne in heavenly glory. All the nations will be gathered before him, and he will separate the people one from another as a shepherd separates the sheep from the goats. He will put the sheep on his right and the goats on his left.

"Then the king will say to those on his right, 'Come, you who are blessed by my father; take your inheritance; the kingdom prepared for you since the creation of the world. For I was hungry and you gave me something to eat, I was thirsty and you gave me something to drink, I was a stranger and you invited me in, I needed clothes and you clothed me, I was sick and you looked after me, I was in prison and you came to visit me.'

"Then the righteous will answer him, 'Lord, when did we see you hungry and feed you or thirsty and give you something to drink? When did we see you a stranger and invite you in or needing clothes and clothe you? When did we see you sick or in prison and go to visit you?'

"The king will reply, 'I tell you the truth. Whatever you did for one of the least of these brothers of mine, you did for me.'"

JESUS CALMS THE STORM

According to the Gospels, one evening, Jesus and his disciples were crossing the Sea of Galilee in a boat. Suddenly, a furious storm came up with the waves breaking over the boat so that it was nearly swamped. Jesus was asleep on a cushion in the stern, and the disciples woke him and asked, "Teacher, don't you care if we drown?"

The Gospel of Mark then states that: He woke up and rebuked the wind, and said to the sea, "Peace! Be still!" Then the wind ceased, and there was a dead calm. He said to them, "Why are you afraid? Have you still no faith?"

And they were filled with great awe and said to one another, "Who then is this that even the wind and the sea obey him?"

This is a story of God's ability to calm the storms in our life and see us through difficult times.

Let's look at the Scriptures in Mark 4:35–41.

Jesus Calms the Storm

That day when evening came, he said to his disciples, "Let us go over to the other side." Leaving the crowd behind, they took him along, just as he was, in the boat. There were also other boats with him. A furious squall came up, and the waves broke over the boat, so that it was nearly swamped. Jesus was in the stern, sleeping on a cushion. The disciples woke him and said to him, "Teacher, don't you care if we drown?"

He got up, rebuked the wind and said to the waves, "Quiet! Be still!" Then the wind died down and it was completely calm.

He said to his disciples, "Why are you so afraid? Do you still have no faith?"

They were terrified and asked each other, "Who is this? Even the wind and the waves obey him!"

Let's examine the story a little closer

Jesus was teaching by the seaside, and there was gathered unto him a great multitude so that he entered into a ship and sat in the ship in the sea, and the whole multitude was by the sea on the land. Jesus said to his disciples that they needed to take the boat to the other side of the sea. Jesus spoke to the crowd in parables; however, he wanted to give his disciples the direct meaning. When Jesus was alone with his disciples, he expounded on the parables to them.

He was also teaching them a lesson in the very journey across the sea. The Bible says that a great storm arose so that all the boats traveling across the sea with him were tossed about by the wind and the waves. Their boat was filling with water, and the disciples began to panic. They woke Jesus up and asked him if he wanted them to drown. That sounds a lot like our prayers when we cry out in desperation in the middle of a storm. We want God to feel sorry for us and calm the storm immediately. Sometimes, the storm is a natural event that we have no control over; and other times, the storm is created by us. Many times, a storm comes in our life so that we will reach out to God.

Jesus was taking a nap on a cushion, and the disciples thought he did not care about their plight. When we pray many times, we think God does not hear us, and at exactly the right time, he answers our prayer. Usually, the answer comes at the very last minute when it seems hopeless, and then God comes through. God has authority over the power of the sea, and he has authority in human affairs. Just as God brings the storms to silence, he also brings peace among the peoples of the earth in their times of need if they call on him.

Jesus looked at the storm and spoke. "Peace, be still." The storm immediately ceased to exist. Jesus then turned to his disciples and asked why they were afraid. Maybe you fear what people think of you: of not having enough money, public speaking, flying, being far from home, spiders, failure or rejection, losing a loved one, disease or pain, and death. These are common fears. We all long to "fear not" to be free to love and be loved. We all long for more of God's peace in the midst of stress, danger, and uncertainty.

The disciples were amazed that the wind and waves obeyed God. Does God have power over the storms in your life? Have you faced challenges that seem insurmountable? We not only face individual storms in our lives but we also face natural disasters and other events that are outside of our control. According to statistics, we face more natural disasters than any time in modern recorded history. Is this yet another sign recorded in the Scriptures prior to the return of the Lord?

Storms and natural disasters today

There were 2,043 storms recorded between 2000 and 2019, including hurricanes, cyclones, and storm surges, killing nearly two hundred thousand people. Storms were the second most frequent disaster type after flooding and the deadliest disaster in the past twenty years. The annual number of "great" earthquakes nearly tripled over the last decade, providing a reminder to Americans that faults like those in the northwest United States might be due for a big one. Between 2004 and 2014, eighteen earthquakes with magnitudes of 8.0 or more rattled continents around the globe. That's an increase of 265 percent over the average rate of the previous century. Wildfires, volcanoes erupting, famine, disease, and war around the globe affect all of us.

What does the Bible say about coming out of a storm? "Do not let your hearts be troubled, and do not be afraid. So do not fear, for I am with you; do not be dismayed, for I am your God. I will strengthen you and help you; I will uphold you with my righteous right hand. I sought the LORD, and he answered me; he delivered me from all my fears." You can have peace in the middle of a storm.

Many times, our faith grows when we are challenged, and we become stronger as a result.

The Bible tells us to be strong and courageous; do not be frightened or dismayed for the Lord your God is with you wherever you go. Be strong and bold; have no fear or dread of them because it is the Lord your God who goes before you. He will be with you; he will not fail you or forsake you. This may not seem easy when we are faced with illness, financial loss, or a crisis in our life. It is in these times that we normally cry out to God for help; however, when the crisis ends, we forget to call on God. We should serve God and others not because religion demands it; we should serve God and others because it benefits us and the people we help. We can reach out and help others in times of crisis and fulfill the call that God has for each one of us.

Serving others in times of trouble

We are hardwired to serve. There are biological reasons for why we feel good when we serve others. Medical science has long known that volunteering contributes to better health. Friendship, kindness, and optimism can help you live to one hundred. The conventional thinking that diet and exercise are keys to a healthier life, with convincing arguments and ample evidence that social engagement, kindness, and/or serving do more for longevity. That's counterintuitive for most of us. Having faith and serving others have a great benefit to our physical and mental health. The Bible teaches this very principle.

Diet and exercise are important for our health. It is healthy to eat organic food and to take care of our physical health. It is more important to take care of our emotional and spiritual health. You should look for a purpose in life and walk out that purpose daily. Are you praying for others and serving your community? Do you pray for peace in America and around the world?

The Bible teaches us that helping others in time of need is important. It helps people to recover from loss and tragedy. It also helps us fulfill what God has called us to do. In addition, giving and caring for others helps our own well-being. Caregiving is a biological process in parts of our brain that encourages us to care for others. We are hard-wired to care for our young ones, elderlies, and animals; it contributes to better, stronger communities, which in itself aids survival. There are two aspects of this system: reward-inducing and stress-reducing. When we come together as a community, we are stronger as a result.

Sometimes, when disaster strikes, we are like a boat tossed about in the sea without an anchor; we forget to call on God in times of trouble. We should have hope in God as an anchor to our soul, both sure and steadfast. God is the unwavering anchor of our soul, as the Scriptures state. A time will come when he will call all believers to that blessed place he has prepared for us. A time will come when you and I will die and all our storms will cease. Enjoy life today in the midst of the storm and trust God as an anchor to the storm in your life. Trust your eternal destiny to the God who promises us eternal life and promises us that he will care for us in this life. When we try to change things in our own strength, we fail. According to Scripture, we need to hand our problems over to God and trust him for the results.

Signs of the End Times

We have already discussed many of the signs of the end times in the previous chapters. Christ was clear in his teachings of how God examines the hearts of mankind. He also lays out why he will return to the earth to destroy evil and rule with righteousness. When left to our own devices, we tend to forget about God and be ruled by our own desires. Troubled by events in the world today, many people are asking, "What on earth is happening?" Pandemics, wars, intense weather patterns, social and political unrest—all stoking fear in our hearts. Did Jesus say anything about the times in which we live and the timing of his return?

Jesus told his disciples how to keep an eye out for signs of the end (also known as the Second Coming or the end of the age). Be on the lookout for prosecution, famines, wars, earthquakes, false prophets, an increase of evil, and a decrease of love. The disciples were given instruction to flee from any place that announces false prophets. And when the time was right, a sign would appear in the sky and the Son of Man would come, riding the clouds. The angels would gather up people who had chosen to follow Christ. The disciples weren't satisfied. They wanted more details on how they'd know it was time. Jesus responded with the parable of the fig tree. No one knows the time or day when the Son of Man will come. You know what that means: we must always be prepared.

To emphasize the importance of watchfulness, Jesus told the parable of the unfaithful servant.

Let's read the Scriptures in Matthew 24.

Signs of the End Times

Jesus left the temple and was walking away when his disciples came up to him to call his attention to its buildings. "Do you see all these things?" he asked. "Truly I tell you, not one stone here will be left on another; everyone will be thrown down."

As Jesus was sitting on the Mount of Olives, the disciples came to him privately. "Tell us," they said, "when will this happen, and what will be the sign of your coming and of the end of the age?"

Jesus answered: "Watch out that no one deceives you. For many will come in my name, claiming, 'I am the Messiah,' and will deceive many. You will hear of wars and rumors of wars, but see to it that you are not alarmed. Such things must happen, but the end is still to come. Nation will rise against nation, and kingdom against kingdom. There will be famines and earthquakes in various places. All these are the beginning of birth pains.

"Then you will be handed over to be persecuted and put to death, and you will be hated by all nations because of me. At that time many will turn away from the faith and will betray and hate each other, and many false prophets will appear and deceive many people. Because of the increase of wickedness, the love of most will grow cold, but the one who stands firm to the end will be saved. And this gospel of the kingdom will be preached in the whole world as a testimony to all nations, and then the end will come.

"So when you see standing in the holy place 'the abomination that causes desolation,' spoken of through the prophet Daniel, let the reader understand then let those who are in Judea flee to the mountains. Let no one on the housetop go down to take anything out of the house. Let no one in the field go back to get their cloak. How dreadful it will be in those days for pregnant women and nursing mothers! Pray that your flight will not take place in winter or on the Sabbath. For then there will be great distress, unequaled from the beginning of the world until now—and never to be equaled again.

"If those days had not been cut short, no one would survive, but for the sake of the elect those days will be shortened. At that time if anyone says to you, 'Look, here is the Messiah!' or, 'There he is!' do not believe it. For false messiahs and false prophets will appear and perform great signs and wonders to deceive, if possible, even the elect. See, I have told you ahead of time.

"So if anyone tells you, 'There he is, out in the wilderness,' do not go out; or, 'Here he is, in the inner rooms,' do not believe it. For as lightning that comes from the east is visible even in the west, so will be the coming of the Son of Man. Wherever there is a carcass, there the vultures will gather.

"Immediately after the distress of those days

"'the sun will be darkened,
and the moon will not give its light;
the stars will fall from the sky,
and the heavenly bodies will be shaken.'

"Then will appear the sign of the Son of Man in heaven. And then all the peoples of the earth will mourn when they see the Son of Man coming on the clouds of heaven, with power and great glory. And he will send his angels with a loud trumpet call, and they will gather his elect from the four winds, from one end of the heavens to the other.

"Now learn this lesson from the fig tree: As soon as its twigs get tender and its leaves come out, you know that summer is near. Even so, when you see all these things, you know that it is near, right at the door. Truly I tell you, this generation will certainly not pass away until all these things have happened. Heaven and earth will pass away, but my words will never pass away.

The Day and Hour Unknown

"But about that day or hour no one knows, not even the angels in heaven, nor the Son, but only the Father. As it was in the days of Noah, so it will be at the coming of the Son of Man. For in the days before the flood, people were eating and drinking, marrying and giving in marriage, up to the day Noah entered the ark; and they knew nothing about what would happen until the flood came and took them all away. That is how it will be at the coming of the Son of Man. Two men will be in the field; one will be taken and the other left. Two women will be grinding with a hand mill; one will be taken and the other left.

"Therefore keep watch, because you do not know on what day your Lord will come. But understand this: If the owner of the house had known at what time of night the thief was coming, he would have kept watch and would not have let his house be broken into. So you also must be ready, because the Son of Man will come at an hour when you do not expect him.

"Who then is the faithful and wise servant, whom the master has put in charge of the servants in his household to give them their food at the proper time? It will be good for that servant whose master finds him doing so when he returns. Truly I tell you, he will put him in charge of all his possessions. But suppose that servant is wicked and says to himself, 'My master is staying away a long time,' and he then begins to beat his fellow servants and to eat and drink with drunkards. The master of that servant will come on a day when he does not expect him and at an hour he is not aware of. He will cut him to pieces and assign him a place with the hypocrites, where there will be weeping and gnashing of teeth.

The world today

Many have suggested that because there were wars in the past that recent wars are not an indicator that this is a sign of the end times. This expectation of the Apocalypse is nothing new. The early Christians expected Jesus Christ to return at any moment and considered the events of their day as evidence of the impending Apocalypse. We obviously know that the expectations of the early Christians turned out to be incorrect, but we rarely look at our own expectations with the same critical eye. Armageddon! The name has inspired books, movies, and an almost endless amount of commentary. The very name conjures up pictures of vast armies, horrible suffering, and widespread devastation. It has created a host of speculations and much embellishment that is not scriptural. How much is known of this great event in the world's history? How much of what is heard can be believed? Have the prophets really spoken that much about it? What about modern prophets? Have they too spoken of it? Where does it get its name? Why would we think the end of the church age is nearer today than any other time in history? What are the signs?

Wars and rumors of war

World War I was fought over Germany, declaring war on Russia and France. Germany's violation of Belgian neutrality and British fears of German domination in Europe brought Britain and its empire into the war. These actions reflect the fears, anxieties and ambitions of the European powers.

World War I, also called First World War or Great War, an international conflict that in 1914–1918 embroiled most of the nations of Europe along with Russia, United States, Middle East, and other regions. The war pitted the Central Powers—mainly Germany, Austria-Hungary, and Turkey—against the Allies, mainly France, Great Britain, Russia, Italy, Japan, and, from 1917, United States. It ended with the defeat of the Central Powers. The war was virtually unprecedented in the slaughter, carnage, and destruction it caused.

World War II, also called Second World War, a conflict that involved virtually every part of the world during the years 1939 to 1945. The principals were the Axis powers: Germany, Italy, and Japan and the Allies: France, Great Britain, United States, Soviet Union, and, to a lesser extent, China. The war was in many respects a continuation, after an uneasy twenty-year hiatus, of the disputes left unsettled by World War I.

The war was fought over freedom and against world domination of an ideal that would have changed the destiny of the world forever. We did not learn a lesson from those wars. We are implementing the same forms of socialism, hatred, religious, and political divisions in our own country and around the world that brought those countries to war. The forty million to fifty million deaths incurred in World War II make it the bloodiest conflict, as well as the largest war, in history.

Rumors of war

After World War II, the Cold War was a period of increased tensions and competition for global influence between the United States that lasted from approximately 1945 until 1991. Tensions increased in the aftermath of World War II when the United States dropped the atom bomb, and Russian forces took over Eastern Europe.

In more recent times, we fought a war of necessity in the eyes of most of the world in Afghanistan and were followed two years later by a war of choice as the US invaded Iraq and called Iran and North Korea an axis of evil. The Iraq War began on March 20, 2003, when the US, joined by the UK, Australia, and Poland, launched a "shock and awe" bombing campaign. Iraqi forces were quickly overwhelmed as coalition forces swept through the country. The invasion led to the collapse of the Ba'athist government; Saddam Hussein was captured during Operation Red Dawn in December of that same year and executed three years later.

The power vacuum following Saddam's demise and mismanagement by the Coalition Provisional Authority led to widespread civil war between Shias and Sunnis, as well as a lengthy insurgency against coalition forces. Many of the violent insurgent groups were supported by Iran and Al-Qaeda in Iraq. The United States responded with a buildup of 170,000 troops in 2007. This buildup gave greater control to Iraq's government and military and was judged a success by many.

After nearly two decades of war, military forces were withdrawn from Afghanistan. The Taliban, a terrorist organization, seized control with menacing swiftness as the Afghan government and security forces that the United States and its allies had spent two decades trying to build collapsed. The United States and its allies spent trillions of dollars fighting a war that could never be won. The religious factions and tribes in those regions had been fighting wars against each other for over a thousand years.

Russia invades Ukraine

Russia's invasion of Ukraine is the biggest military mobilization in Europe since World War II. Here's a guide to how it came about and what's at stake for Russia, US, and NATO.

It felt like a scene from the Cold War, a perilous episode from a bygone era. An unpredictable Russian leader was amassing troops and tanks on a neighbor's border. There was fear of a bloody East-West conflagration. Vladimir Putin ordered Russian forces to invade Ukraine. The repercussions are immediate and far-reaching.

The launch of Russia's full-scale invasion on February 24, 2022, is the largest mobilization of forces Europe has seen since 1945 is underway. So far, Moscow has been denied the swift victory it anticipated and has failed to capture major cities across the country, including Kyiv, the capital. It has been weighed down by an ill-prepared military and has faced tenacious resistance from Ukrainian soldiers and civilian resistance fighters. Still, Russia has superior military might, and Mr. Putin has indicated that his ultimate goal is to capture Kyiv and topple Ukraine's democratically elected government.

The invasion threatens to destabilize the already volatile post-Soviet region, with serious consequences for the security structure that has governed Europe since the 1990s. Mr. Putin has long lamented the loss of Ukraine and other republics when the Soviet Union broke apart. Now diminishing NATO, the military alliance that helped keep the Soviets in check, appears to be part of his mission. Before invading, Russia made a list of far-reaching demands to reshape that structure positions NATO and the United States rejected. With the war grinding on, US intelligence agencies say Mr. Putin has been frustrated by the slow pace of the military advance, and Russian commanders have been increasingly intensifying indiscriminate attacks on civilian targets and infrastructure and resorting to tactics used in previous wars. The list of Ukrainian cities turned to ruins keeps growing.

The war has unleashed a devastating humanitarian toll and claimed thousands of lives. It has also prompted more than five million to flee Ukraine, spurring what the United Nations has called the fastest-growing refugee crisis since World War II. Will there be a World War III, a final war to end all wars as the Bible predicts? A war between the most powerful nations on earth using hypersonic nuclear missiles, a war so devastating that it destroys a third of all mankind?

Financial disaster

The Great Depression was the worst economic downturn in the history of the industrialized world, lasting from 1929 to 1939. It began after the stock market crash of October 1929, which sent Wall Street into a panic and wiped out millions of investors. Over the next several years, consumer spending and investment dropped, causing steep declines in industrial output and employment as failing companies laid off workers. By 1933, when the Great Depression reached its lowest point, some fifteen-million Americans were unemployed and nearly half the country's banks had failed.

What caused the Great Depression?

Throughout the 1920s, the US economy expanded rapidly, and the nation's total wealth more than doubled between 1920 and 1929, a period dubbed "the Roaring Twenties." The stock market, centered at the New York Stock Exchange on Wall Street in New York City, was the scene of reckless speculation.

What was the Great Recession?

The Great Recession was the sharp decline in economic activity during the late 2000s. It is considered the most significant downturn since the Great Depression. The term Great Recession applies to both the US recession, officially lasting from December 2007 to June 2009, and the ensuing global recession in 2009. The economic slump began when the US housing market went from boom to bust, and large amounts of mortgage-backed securities and derivatives lost significant value.

What caused the Great Recession?

In the wake of the 2001 recession and the World Trade Center attacks of September 11, 2001, the US Federal Reserve pushed interest rates lower in an attempt to maintain economic stability. The Fed held low interest rates through mid-2004. This, combined with federal policy to encourage home ownership, low interest rates helped spark a steep boom in real estate and financial markets.

The economy and markets today

The spread of the coronavirus pandemic and turmoil in the crude oil markets caused the Dow Jones to crash by over 37 percent between February 12 and March 23, 2021. While the markets have recovered considerably since, with the Dow rising by over 30 percent from its March 23 lows driven partly by quick fiscal measures taken by the US government, the worst may not be over yet as the economy slips into what appears to be a deep recession with unemployment also soaring. In this analysis, we compare the ongoing crisis with other historic stock market/economic crises, namely, the Great Depression of 1929 (-89 percent peak-to-bottom decline in Dow Jones), Black Monday of

1987 (-31 percent), the 2000s recession (-34 percent), and the Great Recession of 2007–2008 (-49 percent).

On May 5, 2022, the Dow Jones industrial average sank 1,063 points or 3.12 percent and the S&P 500 dropped 3.56 percent while the tech-heavy Nasdaq fared even worse, tumbling 4.9 percent. It was the worst showing for US stocks since the start of the COVID-19 pandemic in March 2020 when the Dow cratered 1,191 points in its largest drop since the financial crisis of 2007 and 2008. To put that in perspective, the 2020 drop may have rivaled some of the most dramatic drops from the 1929 onset of the Great Depression.

In the book of Revelations, John the Apostle is told by Jesus that the world's financial system will collapse in a very short span of time. While many people disregard the prophecies of the Bible, those who have studied their fulfillment believe that the fall of Babylon will take place as it is written. Some people claim our world is approaching the end times; however, we have no way of knowing when that time will come. What we can do is prepare ourselves for Christ's return whenever it may occur.

Babylon of the Old Testament and the New Testament shared a common downfall. Idol worship was their main sin. Babylon idolized itself, and it did not acknowledge or glorify God in any way. This is no different from today. We are constantly consumed with multiple idols that turn our focus away from God, his faithfulness, and his plan for our lives. Idol worship leads to immorality when you are so consumed with the worship of other gods instead of the one true God. We can become obsessed with worshipping money, careers, economic status, education, or politics. When you become focused on striving for success in these areas and not on God, you begin to rely on their role in your life rather than God's provision.

Is cryptocurrency a sign of a one-world financial system described in the Bible? From the beginning, bitcoins became the currency of choice for many in the web's black market. They are used to buy and sell drugs, weapons, and stolen art and to engage in human trafficking. Many who engage in ransomware (viruses that threaten to delete the information on your computer unless you pay) demand payment in bitcoins. They are also popular with people who wish to gamble online on overseas sites (which is illegal in the US) or donate to charities the government doesn't approve of (like Wikileaks). But, over the years, more reputable businesses have accepted bitcoin payment, including the video game platform Steam, Overstock.com, Microsoft, and Tesla.

The idea of a one-world currency is vaguely suggested in the Bible. Revelation 13:16–17 say that the Antichrist will require everyone to have the mark of the beast to engage in any financial transactions. It's unknown what exactly this mark will be, but it's entirely possible that some kind of cryptocurrency will be involved. That would certainly be more efficient than printing and distributing a standardized physical currency all over the world. It's possible that the mark of the beast will be what allows people to access the cryptocurrency in their virtual accounts. One man in Iceland has already implanted a chip in his hand to access his bitcoins.

Plagues and pestilence

The world would be convulsed by another deadly event. In January 1918, a new strain of flu began making its way across the globe. The origin of the virus remains unknown. Some historians have theorized that the virus originated in a British camp in France while others are convinced it came from North America. However, as the virus spread, the heavily censored press on both sides of World War I suppressed the news of the outbreak in fear that it would damage morale. In neutral Spain, the uncensored press was free to publish news of a deadly disease that had swept the country, a phenomenon which led to the virus being given its name: Spanish flu.

The Spanish flu emerged at a time when the world was becoming increasingly interconnected, thanks to the realities of World War I. Troops on both sides coming to and from the front lines easily spread the disease to civilians. The Spanish flu thrived in urban population centers and soon spread to the countryside, leaving few places in the world untouched by the medieval-style plague. Businesses and schools closed. Quarantines were enforced. People donned face masks as they went about their daily business. These measures, however, seemed ineffectual in stemming the tide of the disease. After three waves over the course of eighteen months, an estimated third of the world's population was affected, with as many as fifty million people dead as a result of the virus. While the Spanish flu tended to kill the very young and the very old, those of median age also suffered tremendously.

In 2019, another devastating pandemic would strike. World deaths from COVID-19 have now officially reached five million (with experts estimating a much higher toll). India, Brazil, Iran, France, Turkey, and Russia follow the US as among the countries leading in infection rates. The infection rate in India exploded, overwhelming the health system as a second wave created a record daily number of infections before subsiding. Elsewhere in the world, Indonesia became a major hot spot while other countries in Asia, Africa, and Latin America are seeing alarming increases in infection rates and deaths with the spread of more virulent variants (the delta variant, the most prevalent, and now a new delta subvariant). As the US and other countries in the West struggle to emerge from the pandemic, countries and communities with limited access to vaccines are facing new threats from COVID-19 as more health systems are overwhelmed by rising infection rates.

US resurgence

On September 20, 2021, the US marked another grim milestone in the fight against COVID-19, recording more American deaths from COVID-19 than the Spanish flu in 1918—making COVID-19 the deadliest pandemic in American history.

The Bible speaks of similar signs prior to the return of the Lord.

Signs of the End Times

The Apostle Paul, in writing his very last letter, warned Timothy "that in the last days, there will come times of severe difficulty." He is telling him the state of man and the behavior that will be displayed prior to the return of Christ. He said people will be lovers of self, lovers of money, proud, arrogant, abusive, disobedient to their parents, ungrateful, unholy, heartless, unappeasable, slanderous, without self-control, brutal, and not loving good. That sounds very much like a lack of love in people today, and we've seen that in the last few years. It will not get better but will only grow worse. As violent movies and video games increase, we are becoming desensitized to violence. Some of the video games and movies are so heinous now that we are becoming accustomed to it; now we want more even worse violence and try to top the last thrill.

Today, human life is seen as disposable, killing in the streets of major American cities. Police killings caused riots in the streets, and cities were burned as a result. The homicide rate and crime are rising in American cities. Homicide increase isn't happening at random, but much of the additional violence is clustered in disadvantaged neighborhoods that were already struggling with higher rates of gun violence than before the pandemic. Random violence and terrorism seem to be rampant around the world. Hatred seems to be at an all-time high. Random crimes and murder take place every day over the most trivial matters. The impact is especially severe on children who are continually exposed to violent crime from an early age.

Paul speaks about this when he said that the time is coming; perhaps, the time has already come "when people will not endure sound teaching, but having itching ears they will accumulate for themselves teachers to suit their own passions and will turn away from listening to the truth and wander off into myths." Since they are following "their own passions" of sex, violence, and hatred, they will turn away from the truth and live a life devoid of God.

Signs in the heavens

Christ did mention some physical signs that would be visible in the heavens: "Immediately after the tribulation of those days the sun will be darkened, and the moon will not give its light; the stars will fall from heaven, and the powers of the heavens will be shaken." Note that this is immediately after a difficult time known as the tribulation and just before his physical return. "Then the sign of the Son of Man will appear in heaven, and then all the tribes of the earth will mourn, and they will see the Son of Man coming on the clouds of heaven with power and great glory." While there will be signs in the heavens before Christ's return, these occur just prior to his return and after the great tribulation.

The world will end, and Jesus spoke about the end of the world. He explained how the earth would one day pass away. He also shared that there would be an increase in earthquakes, famines, wars, and pandemics before the end. But in the book of Revelation, the apostle John shared how God would then create a new heaven and new earth.

How it all will happen is a mystery. Jesus was very clear that no one knows when the end will come. He explained that he would one day return at a time that no one expects, like a thief in the night. Followers of Jesus are therefore encouraged to "be ready."

Jesus promised help to face the everyday challenges of life. Believers were never promised to have fewer troubles than other people. However, Jesus did promise to help those who ask him for help through any and every trouble of life. Nothing you will ever face in your life can surprise God, not even the end of the world.

What if the God of the universe really does have a plan for your life? It's impossible to know whether or not we're living in the end times. However, we have an opportunity to follow and trust in the God who does know the end from the beginning. God promises to be present and help you no matter what happens in your life.

CHRIST DIED FOR US

In Exodus 4:22, the Israelites, as a people of God, were called "my firstborn son" by God using the singular form to refer to all his people. In the Gospel of John, the focus shifted to the person of Jesus as the representative of that title being the Son of God. The verse is part of the New Testament narrative in the third chapter of John in the discussion at Jerusalem between Jesus and Nicodemus, who was called a "ruler of the Jews."

In John 3:3, Jesus spoke of the necessity of a man being born again before he could "see the kingdom of God." Jesus spoke also of "heavenly things" (in verses 11–13) and of salvation (in verses 14–17) and the condemnation (in verses 18–19) of those who do not believe in Jesus. "And as Moses lifted up the serpent in the wilderness, even so must the Son of man be lifted up: That whosoever believeth in him should not perish, but have eternal life" (John 3:14–15).

Jesus Christ's death by crucifixion was reserved for the worst of criminals. His death on the cross was a necessary sacrifice for the atonement of our sins. Atonement was needed because of the depravity of man (Romans 1–3). The LORD God is a holy God, and he cannot look upon sin.

Atonement in Judaism

The Hebrew word "kaphar" in the Old Testament Bible is translated into English as "atonement," and it means "to cover." Atonement involved the sacrifice of an innocent animal, and by the shed blood of that animal, God would see the sins of the person(s) who offered the sacrifice covered. It was the process of causing a transgression to be forgiven or pardoned. In Rabbinic Judaism, people achieved atonement through repentance, sometimes followed by some combination of confession, restitution, tribulations (unpleasant life experiences), the experience of dying, or other factors.

Another aspect of atonement is the occurrence of Yom Kippur (the day itself, as distinct from the temple service performed on it), also known as the Day of Atonement, which is a biblical/Jewish observance.

Atonement, in Christianity, describes beliefs that human beings can be reconciled to God through Christ's sacrificial suffering and death. The "blood of Christ" is a clear expression for the death of Christ. Blood is the symbol of sacrificial death, a life poured out in death. It is not the releasing of life but the end of the life—death. Redemption is only possible by blood life poured out. Hebrews 9:22 summarizes the whole Old Testament teaching on sacrifice. "And according to the Law, one may almost say, all things are cleansed with blood, and without shedding of blood there is no forgiveness." Atonement refers to the forgiving or pardoning of sin and original sin, in particular, through the suffering, death, and resurrection of Jesus. The New

Testament emphasizes that Jesus is the Savior of the world, and through his death, the sins of humanity have been forgiven, enabling the reconciliation between God and his creation.

Why did the Jewish and Roman leaders and the community want Christ to die?

The Jewish leaders wanted Jesus to die because they believed they had the truth. In fact, they did have the truth, and under the Law of Moses, they served the true and living God. Man had, however, corrupted the original law to benefit the ruling class. Their law also spoke of a Messiah who would come and redeem them from the law and sin. The very Scriptures spelled out who Christ was, and they overlooked him because they wanted a different kind of savior. The common people wanted him killed because they were convicted of their sin. They wanted the miracles and the provisions; however, they drew the line at giving up their sin. Both were guilty of his condemnation. God knew this would happen, and in a sense, they helped complete the work described in the Old Testament that Christ would die for their sins. In Jesus's case, it seemed just about everyone contributed. The Jewish religious leaders, the Gentile Roman government, and a mob of people all demanded his death.

The ministry of Christ?

It all started in a small village, not far from Jerusalem, in Israel. At thirty years of age, Jesus began teaching people about life and God.

Crowds were drawn to him. Everything about Jesus was markedly different from the ruling religious leaders. He welcomed not only the wealthy and powerful but also the prostitutes, poor, diseased, and marginalized.

Jesus called people to believe in him, saying things like, "I am the light of the world. He who follows me will not walk in darkness but will have the light of life."

Why did people listen to Jesus?

It was because of what they saw.

Jesus went throughout all the cities and villages, teaching in their synagogues, proclaiming the Gospel of the kingdom and healing every disease and every affliction. The blind could see, the lame could walk, and lepers were free from leprosy. He fed a destitute crowd of four thousand people, starting with a handful of fish and loaves of bread. He did it again with five thousand people. During a raging storm at sea, Jesus stood and commanded the wind and rain to stop, bringing sudden calm. The men in the boat asked, "Who is this that even the wind and seas obey him?" Several times, he brought dead people back to life. It's no wonder crowds followed Jesus, and word of him spread.

So why was Jesus crucified?

As Jesus taught the crowds, he also was critical of the ruling religious authorities. They flaunted their position, insisting on obedience to their demanding rituals, laws, and traditions. Jesus said of them, "They tie up heavy burdens, hard to bear, and lay them on people's shoulder," and in direct challenge to them he said, "You hypocrites! Well did Isaiah prophesy of you when he said, 'This people honor me with their lips, but their heart is far from me; in vain do they worship me, teaching as doctrines the commandments of men.'" For example, one of their religious laws regarded no work on the Sabbath: no cooking, no walking a certain distance, no carrying any objects, etc. It was more restrictive than restful.

On a Sabbath day, Jesus healed a man who was blind from birth. He saved a Samaritan woman who had no standing in society and made her an evangelist. He forgave the sins of an adulterous woman and convicted the hearts of those who condemned her. He fed five thousand people with two fish and five loaves of bread. He calmed the storm in the middle of the sea when all hope was lost. He healed a woman who had spent all her resources on doctors who could not heal her. He provided money for Peter to pay his taxes. He constantly was healing people, raising people from the dead, forgiving the sins of people who were thought beyond hope. He did not stop working on the Sabbath. When the Pharisees confronted Jesus for working (healing people) on the Sabbath, Jesus said, "My Father is working until now, and I am working." We're told, "This was why the Jews were seeking all the more to kill him because not only was he breaking the Sabbath but he was even calling God his own father, making himself equal with God."

Why we need Christ

Everyone experiences pain in their lifetime. No one asks to be hurt. Yet pain is commonplace in our lives. Our pain is the direct result of sin in the world. It is because of that sin that we experience pain and are separated from God. However, there is still hope for us, and that hope is through Jesus Christ. God came down from heaven as the man Jesus, lived a perfect life, and then died an innocent death on the cross so that we could live a free and peaceful life with him. The Bible says that he went to the cross as a sacrifice for our sins and as a substitute for us. Yes, he took our place so we would not receive eternal punishment but rather receive eternal life.

Jesus was clear about his deity

Jesus said to know him was to know God, to see him was to see God, to believe in him was to believe in God, to receive him was to receive God, to hate him was to hate God, and to honor him was to honor God.

A Conversation with Nicodemus

Nicodemus was a Pharisee and a member of the Jewish council. He came to Jesus one night and said to him, "Rabbi, we know that God has sent you as a teacher. No one can perform the miracles you perform unless God is with him."

Jesus replied to Nicodemus, "I can guarantee this truth: No one can see God's kingdom without being born from above."

Nicodemus asked him, "How can anyone be born when he's an old man? He can't go back inside his mother a second time to be born, can he?"

Jesus answered, "Nicodemus, I can guarantee this truth: No one can enter God's kingdom without being born of water and the Spirit. Flesh and blood give birth to flesh and blood, but the Spirit gives birth to things that are spiritual. Don't be surprised when I tell you that all of you must be born from above. The wind blows wherever it pleases. You hear its sound, but you don't know where the wind comes from or where it's going. That's the way it is with everyone born of the Spirit."

Nicodemus replied, "How can that be?"

Jesus told Nicodemus, "You're a well-known teacher of Israel. Can't you understand this? I can guarantee this truth: We know what we're talking about, and we confirm what we've seen. Yet, you don't accept our message. If you don't believe me when I tell you about things on earth, how will you believe me when I tell you about things in heaven? No one has gone to heaven except the Son of Man, who came from heaven.

"As Moses lifted up the snake [on a pole] in the desert, so the Son of Man must be lifted up. Then everyone who believes in him will have eternal life."

God loved the world this way: He gave his only Son so that everyone who believes in him will not die but will have eternal life. God sent his Son into the world, not to condemn the world, but to save the world. Those who believe in him won't be condemned. But those who don't believe are already condemned because they don't believe in God's only Son.

This is why people are condemned: The light came into the world. Yet, people loved the dark rather than the light because their actions were evil. People who do what is wrong hate the light and don't come to the light. They don't want

their actions to be exposed. But people
who do what is true come to the light so
that the things they do for God may be
clearly seen. (John 3:1–21)

Let's look at the Scriptures a little closer

Nicodemus was a leader of the Jews and a teacher of
Jewish law. He came to Jesus for answers. He and the Jewish
leaders admitted that Jesus was sent from God because they
admitted that no one could perform the miracles that Jesus
performed without God. Nicodemus called Jesus "rabbi"
because of his teachings and the power that comes from
God displayed in the works that Jesus performed.

Jesus told Nicodemus that he came from heaven and
that Nicodemus must be born again to enter the kingdom
of God. Nicodemus was perplexed at the saying and questioned Jesus further. "Can a man enter his mother's womb
a second time when he is old?" Jesus responded that to
enter the kingdom of God, we must be born of water and
spirit. Jesus explained that once you accept Christ as your
Lord and Savior, the Holy Spirit comes to live in you and
transforms your life. Jesus also explained that we must be
baptized to represent him cleansing us from sin.

"For God so loved the world that he gave his one and
only Son, that whoever believes in him shall not perish
but have eternal life. For God did not send his Son into
the world to condemn the world, but to save the world
through him" (John 3:16–17). Jesus explained that he was
God's only son and that whoever would believe in him

would have eternal life. He explained that he did not come into the world from heaven to condemn the world but to save the world. He went on to explain that whoever would reject Christ would also reject eternal life.

The Scriptures also tell us how to accept Christ. Romans 10:9–10 says, "If you declare with your mouth, 'Jesus is Lord,' and believe in your heart that God raised him from the dead, you will be saved. For it is with your heart that you believe and are justified, and it is with your mouth that you profess your faith and are saved." It is as simple as confessing that Christ died for your sins and accepting him as your Lord and Savior.

Acts 2:38 says, "Repent and be baptized, every one of you, in the name of Jesus Christ for the forgiveness of your sins. And you will receive the gift of the Holy Spirit." When we receive Christ as our Lord and Savior and are baptized, the Bible says that we are filled with his Holy Spirit. "His Holy Spirit seals us for the day of redemption and works in our life to transform us into the very image of Christ" (Ephesians 4:30).

Jesus then explained to Nicodemus the work of the Holy Spirit. He told him that much like the wind, we could see and feel the effects; however, we could not see the wind. Lifestyle changes are a result of focus and practice. The one who looks at God's word intently and puts it into effect will be blessed. It is one thing to define an experience and another thing to walk in it. To walk in it, you must focus on it and intentionally practice it for a while until it becomes a natural, instinctive part of your life.

Jesus went on to explain that he must die on the cross to redeem all from their sins and eternal damnation. God has provided a way for us to live and not suffer eternal death and damnation, as he promised Adam and Eve that seed of the woman (Christ) would crush the serpent's head. Adam and Eve had fallen into sin by deception with no hope of salvation and were told by God that they needed to look forward to the work of the cross.

As Moses lifted up the serpent in the wilderness that all who, in faith, looked to it could live. The people of God in the wilderness following Moses also fell into sin, and many died as a result. God instructed Moses to fashion a serpent on a wooden pole and lift it up, and anyone who looked upon it would live. God was also pointing them to Christ that he would be lifted up on a cross for their sin. Likewise, if we look to Christ who was crucified and became sin for us, we also will be saved by the redemptive work of the cross if we simply believe by faith. God sent his only begotten son into the world. Jesus was the seed of the woman spoken of in the Bible in the book of Genesis. Likewise, the law was given to Moses so we would know what sin is. God wanted us to know that no one could live a perfect life under the law and therefore redeem themselves from sin.

Jesus, Son of God and Son of man, was lifted up when he was crucified and condemned upon the cross for the sins of the whole world. We are still bitten by the old evil serpent and have the poison of sin flowing through our hearts and veins. God, in his great love for all mankind, sent his only begotten son into the world not to condemn us for our sin but to bear our punishment and save us from eternal death and damnation.

Jesus explained that he must be crucified to redeem us from our sin and that we needed to accept the redemptive work of the cross to receive eternal life. Sinners today can look to Christ Jesus, who was crucified for our sins and had risen again in victory; and those who look to Jesus in faith will not die eternally but live! Jesus used the example of Moses lifting up a pole (tree) in the wilderness with a serpent (the deception of Satan and sin) as an example of Christ being lifted up on the cross to die for our sins.

Jesus, when he was lifted up upon the cross, paid in full the just penalty for the sins of all people. His resurrection is proof. Those who look to Jesus in faith will not be condemned to hell for their sins; for in Jesus, God graciously forgives their sins and give them everlasting life instead. In Jesus, we who should die for our sins are given everlasting life in the glories of heaven. How great God's love toward us is in Christ Jesus!

To be saved, one must confess with his mouth that Jesus is Lord and also believe it in their heart. A simple prayer like this is sufficient to invite Jesus into your heart and life:

Dear Jesus,

I have sinned and turned aside from loving, trusting, and honoring you with my life. Do not deal with me as I deserve on account of my sin. I look to you and

your cross for salvation. Forgive my sin,
cleanse my heart, and grant me life eternal with you in your everlasting kingdom.
Amen.

If you said that simple prayer, I believe you are born
again. Welcome to the kingdom of God.

Jesus then explained to Nicodemus why people rejected
him. He explained that mankind would rather live in
deception rather than have their deeds exposed. The Holy
Spirit transforms our hearts and life if we allow; however,
we must allow Christ, the light of God, in our heart for it
to be examined. Many enjoy their sin and the pleasures of
their life too much to have their life changed.

*There was a man of the Pharisees, named Nicodemus, a ruler
of the Jews.*

Nicodemus was a ruler of the Jews and would have
been ashamed to be seen with Christ. Nicodemus was a
teacher of the law given by Moses and wanted to find out
if Jesus really was the Messiah sent by God. He was most
likely afraid of what the other teachers thought. He obviously wanted salvation through Christ; however, he was
more concerned about his leadership position. Are you too
cool or too intelligent to be seen in church? Nicodemus
wanted a new start, and Jesus welcomed him. After talking
with Jesus, Nicodemus came to faith in Christ. When he
was faced with concerns about the salvation of his own

soul, he was willing to walk away from the only religion he had known.

Jesus spoke to Nicodemus about regeneration or a new birth by the Holy Spirit. Jesus explained that the Holy Spirit was the true source of holiness and gave us a new life. Jesus told Nicodemus that he could begin life again. Do you desire a new start in life? A life devoid of the previous mistakes? A new life filled with purpose? God will give you a new heart with new desires and a new sense of direction.

By our first birth, we were born into sin with a corrupt, fallen nature. This new birth from heaven also known as salvation gives us a new beginning. The Holy Spirit will cause change that we ourselves are unable to obtain. He will give us a new nature and a new heart. We must first admit that we are a sinner and confess that very thing. Repentance means a change of mind or thought that leads to a change of action. Salvation is a result of true repentance.

Salvation is looking to the eternal destiny, a destiny that lasts forever. Each of our souls requires the change, and the change is necessary for transition into eternity. There is a great change in the heart of the sinner when true regeneration takes place with the help of the Holy Spirit. You see, the journey into eternity begins the moment you are born again. Now we live a new direction with a change of character. As we begin to study his word and pray, God will give you his wisdom and help guide you through life. He will reveal to you who he intended you to be and give you a desire to follow a path that he is calling you to when we study the word of God and pray for direction. True happiness and success only comes from God and knowing that you have eternal security with him.

Christ referred to the ordinance of baptism. Not that all those and those only who are baptized are saved, but without that new birth, which is brought by the Spirit and then signified by baptism. Jesus said like the wind blowing, so the Spirit of God directs us. The Spirit sends his influences wherever, whenever, whomever, and whatever measure he desires. Though the causes are hidden, the effects are plain when the soul is brought to mourn for sin and to breathe after Christ. Christ is teaching the doctrine of regeneration and its necessity in our life. Thus, the things of the Spirit and of God are foolishness to the natural man.

Jesus was telling us that he is the Lord of our life, and we must be taught and saved by him. He said that whoever would believe in Christ, should not perish but should have everlasting life. God was in Christ, reconciling the world to himself and saving it. It could only be saved through him; there is no salvation in any other. He said that he who believeth in Christ would not be condemned.

SAVED BY GRACE

People will often try to comfort those who realize their shortcomings by saying something like, "Don't be afraid—God knows your heart." In attempting to comfort people we, many times, fail to tell them the truth. The truth is that our only hope is to place our faith in Jesus Christ who lived a perfect life, died on the cross to pay for our sins, and rose again. Our sin is imputed to him, and his righteousness is imputed to us when we trust him (2 Corinthians 5:21). We are justified not by our works (Romans 3:20) but by Jesus's resurrection (Romans 4:25). Faith is repenting of our sin, admitting that we are hopelessly and helplessly lost and unable to do anything to gain God's favor, and then simply accepting the salvation that he offers freely. We are saved by grace; the work is God's, not ours.

Maybe you are an intellectual, and you think you need to understand God before you can accept him. Maybe you have tried all the other religions to no avail. So here is a test for you: pray and ask God if he is real. There is no loss in asking God for his help. There is no shame in not knowing the answers. Ask God to show you he is real; if nothing happens, then you have nothing to lose. However, if he is real and he reveals himself to you and you reject him, you have everything to lose.

Why did God provide only one way to heaven? Wouldn't it have been more "user-friendly" to create many paths leading to eternity with him?

In an attempt to illustrate God's perfect plan, I picture a kingdom on a mountain. There is one road to the summit, leading right to the kingdom's gates. A free map (the Bible) is offered to anyone who asks. Yet most people do not follow the map. The road to the kingdom (heaven) is narrow and not always easy to navigate. Instead, the travelers choose other roads. Wide and easy, with beautiful scenery on the way, they convince themselves that the road they're on must lead to the kingdom! However, those paths never reach the gates. At some point, they either take a detour or simply reach a dead end and never reach the kingdom.

What does the Bible say about salvation?

Ephesians 2:8–9 say, "For it is by grace you have been saved, through faith, and this is not from yourselves, it is the gift of God not by works, so that no one can boast." According to the Scriptures, you are unable to accept God other than by faith. It is not through our human intellect that we accept God. We also cannot earn our way into heaven by our good deeds.

There is much misunderstanding about being saved by grace. A great many who call themselves Christians assume that the grace of God has established a system whereby the sinner can mitigate his deserved punishment by his own efforts. For some, this may be a formal system of sacraments that infuse the soul with the grace of God. For others, the system is less formal but still includes various religious activities, such as, church attendance, baptism, contributing to the offering, and doing good deeds. While most agree that "nobody's perfect," many say that God in his "grace" will overlook our sins if he sees that we have made a genuine effort to do the right thing, mend our ways, and avail ourselves of the help he offers through the church. We think if God sees that the trajectory of our lives is headed in the right direction, then in his "grace," he will forgive our sins and grant us eternal life. In this view of "grace," the sinner does not earn eternal life in an absolute sense, but his penitent response and genuine effort do trigger a gracious response from the Father. This belief, although widespread, contradicts the true meaning of grace.

So many people believe that because they are good people, they will automatically go to heaven. There is a common perception that so long as one leads a generally good life, they will get into heaven. But the question is: Don't all good people go to heaven? Most people believe that God exists and that he is all-loving. There is, however, an assumption that although some "bad" people may need punishment, most people are generally "good" and, as such, are entitled to heaven. There is the view that the entrance into heaven is on the basis of merit (our works) rather than God's grace. The next assumption is an implicit suggestion that hell, if it exists at all, is really only for a marginal few who are responsible for particularly evil acts.

Do all "good" people go to heaven? Since no one is good as defined by God, the answer is, "No." Those who enter heaven do so not on the basis of merit but on the basis of God's grace as bestowed by Jesus Christ. We can't work our way to heaven or claim to be without sin (1 John 1:8). Instead, we must humbly submit to God, turn from our wrong behavior, and turn to Christ for salvation.

So what is God's grace

A simple answer would be the unmerited favor of God toward sinners who do not deserve salvation. Mercy is forgiving the sinner and withholding the punishment that is justly deserved. Grace is heaping undeserved blessings upon the sinner in salvation. God shows us mercy and grace by offering his son as a sacrifice for our sin. The complicated answer is that grace has been defined as the divine influence that operates in humans to regenerate and sanctify the soul, to inspire virtuous impulses, and to impart strength to endure trials and resist temptation; and as an individual, God gives us virtue and excellence of divine origin.

Have you ever run out of gas and been stranded on the side of the road? You then had to wait for a ride or walk to a gas station to refuel the vehicle before it would go. So many times, Christians neglect their faith, forget to pray or read the bible, and neglect fellowship with other believers, and then we run out of the empowerment of the Holy Spirit. The trials of life begin to get us down, and we forget to refuel. When we forget to rely on God, we lack the power to move forward in his perfect will. Our focus without the

Holy Spirit is then concentrated on the problems rather than the answers.

The Bible says that his grace is sufficient to carry us through the trails of life. In 2 Corinthians 12:9, it says, "But he said to me, 'My grace is sufficient for you, for my power is made perfect in weakness.' Therefore I will boast all the more gladly about my weaknesses, so that Christ's power may rest on me." That is why, for Christ's sake, I delight in weaknesses, in insults, in hardships, in persecutions, and in difficulties.

The Bible does not say that we will not face many trials; however, it does say that God will be with you through the trials. As a result of the trial, we gain character and strength if we rely on the Holy Spirit. You also gain patience and endurance for the next trial that comes your way. Now you have experience in trusting God through difficult situations, and you can help another who is facing a similar trial.

> As a prisoner for the Lord, then, I urge you to live a life worthy of the calling you have received. Be completely humble and gentle; be patient, bearing with one another in love. Make every effort to keep the unity of the Spirit through the bond of peace. There is one body and one Spirit, just as you were called to one hope when you were called; one Lord, one faith, one baptism; one God and Father of

all, who is over all and through all and in
all. (Ephesians 4:1–6)

The Apostle Paul compared his relationship with God
as a prisoner of the Lord. Paul restrained himself from acting out in his flesh to benefit the kingdom of God. He
commanded us to be completely humble and gentle, to be
patient, and to bear one another in love. How many of us
have that kind of strength? We have the strength to benefit
others and the kingdom of God by humbling ourselves and
trusting God no matter how difficult the trial. Paul also
stated that we are to keep peace with all Christians regardless of whether we agree with them or not. He said that
there is one body—meaning, the church—one faith, one
hope, and one baptism.

Every virtue in a Christian's life begins and ends with
Christ's love. Being humble is challenging unless we have
accepted Christ into our lives as our Savior. By accepting
Christ into our hearts, we are filled with the Holy Spirit
and the overwhelming love of God. Unless we have "God's
love" in our hearts and souls, it is impossible to be "truly
humble" and show "true grace" to others.

As sinners, we are much more likely to act pride-
fully, opinionatedly, egotistically, judgmentally, enviously,
fault-findingly, arrogantly, disdainfully, haughtily, covet-
ingly, greedily, spitefully, autocratically, hardheadedly, and
vainly rather than humbly. As humans, we "naturally" act
sinful without God's help.

In James 4:6, it says, "But he gives us more grace if we
are humble. That is why Scripture says: 'God opposes the

proud but shows favor to the humble.'" Humility is the fundamental law for all salvation, and now it has become crystal clear for me that in the deepest sense, this is one of the most important biblical principles. God gives grace to the humble, and what people think about you doesn't matter. The proud, the high-minded, the arrogant, and those who are wise in their own eyes have God as their opponent.

You only receive as much grace as the humility you possess. You may notice at times that there is little progress at all in your life. Is it because you are not receiving God's grace? You can accomplish a lot in your own human strength. You can attempt to compensate for a lack of grace by being zealous in many things. You can be capable and good as a human being, but all that human goodness and ability doesn't help a bit if God opposes you. If you are not willing to admit that you make mistakes, then you aren't acknowledging your sin. And you aren't judging yourself, but you are defending yourself to God instead.

Many times, people are hurt by people in church and religious people. Church is not a showcase of the perfection of saints, but it is a hospital for the broken and hurting. I had a man who came to Bible study because his friend came. He interrupted the study with a barrage of questions. He didn't want the answers; he just wanted to interfere. I asked if he could wait until the end of the preplanned lesson so the others could learn, and then I would answer the questions and take all the time he needed. He had religion forced on him as a child and rebelled against any form of organized religion. He returned the following week, and we spent time in the Scriptures together. Week after week, he learned what the Bible taught. His family started attending church. They wanted to know what happened to Uncle Dave. He was a hard-hearted man who was abrupt with everyone. God slowly began to change his heart, and everyone noticed the difference. All Dave needed was a friend. Once he discovered what the Bible said and began to live by it, he changed. He became a dear friend to me and all the members of the church.

Without the grace of God, we are unable to live victoriously in this life. However, we are not without his grace! His grace is what enables us to overcome any obstacle we may face. We have already been given everything we need to live in victory! It doesn't matter what may come against us; we are more than conquerors with the grace of God. We are meant to be courageous in faith that his grace will carry us through difficult times.

THE GREAT COMMISSION

The Bible tells us to join with other believers to learn and grow in our faith (Hebrews 10:25). Whether it is in a church, a Bible study, a small group, or even with a friend, we all need the encouragement of others to strengthen us.

The Scriptures say, "But encourage one another daily, as long as it is called today, so that none of you may be hardened by sin's deceitfulness." In 1 Thessalonians 5:11, it says, "Therefore encourage one another and build each other up, just as in fact you are doing." Throughout the Bible, we see instructions to encourage one another and verses that are meant to encourage us. Why is encouragement emphasized in the Bible? We do this primarily because encouragement is necessary to our walk of faith.

The Bible also tells us to gather together to worship God and learn of him. The Scriptures say, "Not forsaking the assembling of ourselves together, as is the manner of some, but exhorting one another, and so much the more as you see the Day approaching."

The Bible also commands us to go into the entire world to preach the Gospel of Jesus Christ and make disciples of all mankind (Matthew 28:19–20). Jesus gave what is known today as the Great Commission, which is to "go therefore and make disciples of all the nations, baptizing them in the name of the Father and of the Son and of the Holy Spirit, teaching them to observe all things that I have commanded you."

Mark 1:17 says, "'Come, follow me,' Jesus said, 'and I will send you out to fish for people.'" The phrase "fishers of men" in Mark 1:17 is one of the most well-known lines in the entire New Testament and the most important metaphor for evangelism. The image probably had an important role in the adoption of the ichthus as a symbol of early Christianity. The reference has also often been moved from the disciples to Jesus, with him being called the "fisher of men," and the image of Jesus as a fisherman is second only to that of Jesus as a shepherd.

But here is what is often left out of the Great Commission: "Make disciples of all nations." Every Christian is called to go into the world and make disciples. I didn't say that everyone is called to be a preacher. Not everyone is called to be a great evangelist. You might be a behind-the-scenes person, a little shy, but you can still spread your faith through social media or simply share your faith with a friend. You might be someone who is a little timid, but you can let people know that you are a person of faith. Who knows? You may spark a conversation that leads someone to Christ. You never know that person you witness to may be the one who'll go on to preach the Gospel to all nations. However you do it, we are all called to go and make disciples.

There are a lot of Christians today who have never told anyone they believe in Christ. They have never even thought about it, much less made an effort to do it. The way to grow in faith is to share with others and hopefully lead others to Christ. Imagine being in heaven and missing a loved one or a friend who you could have talked to.

The Scriptures command us to make disciples

"Therefore, go and make disciples of all nations, baptizing them in the name of the Father and of the Son and of the Holy Spirit, and teaching them to obey everything I have commanded you. And surely I am with you always, to the very end of the age."

It is important to articulate a Christian worldview for the twenty-first century with all of its accompanying challenges and changes. We need to show how such Christian thinking is applicable across all areas of life. At the heart of these challenges and changes, we see that truth, morality, and interpretive frameworks are being ignored if not rejected. Such challenges are formidable indeed. Throughout culture, the very existence of normative truth is being challenged.

Responding to culture's challenges

For Christians to respond to these challenges, we must hear afresh the words of Jesus from what is called the Great Commandment (Matthew 22:36–40). Here we are told to love God not only with our hearts and souls but also with our minds. Jesus's words refer to a wholehearted devotion to God with every aspect of our being: emotionally, vocationally, or cognitively. This kind of love for God results in taking every thought captive to make it obedient to Christ. This means being able to see life from a Christian vantage point; it means thinking with the mind and heart of Christ.

The Gospel (good news) is the teaching of what Jesus did for us through his life, death, and resurrection. This is the center of Christian faith and the center of who we are as believers. We base all that we do and believe on what God has revealed through his written word, the Bible. We live out the Christian life in dependence on the leading and empowering of the Holy Spirit. It is that example and teaching that brings others to Christ through faith in him.

If we want our friends and neighbors to listen to our story, then we must listen to theirs. If we want others to attend to our convictions, then we must first attend to theirs. If we desire for others to cultivate common ground with us, we must do so first. In doing so, we will create a communication climate in which we can fulfill our deepest longing of engaging others in a respectful, civil way that allows us to share a perspective that has changed our lives.

People are looking for answers, not insults. If we want to share the Gospel of Christ, we must be open to the ideas of others and embrace people for who they are. It is Christ who does the work in the heart of man, but we try to convince people that our way is the only way. In reality, what we need to do is explain why we believe what we believe and leave the choice to them.

Why Christ over intellect and religion

Intellectualism and religiosity are controversial concepts in terms of their relationship. Numerous studies suggest that intelligence and exposure to higher education reduce religiosity. Individuals make a choice when they are young. They choose between holding a certain belief or disbelief. If we are taught that we are only part of the animal hierarchy and that we have no purpose other than just to exist, then we believe that. It is easy for someone who has never had faith or an understanding of biblical teaching to explain God away. If we are taught that God created the heavens and the earth and all things within them, we tend to embrace a biblical worldview. That is why we need to understand the Scriptures to give an account of why we believe.

We have a natural curiosity when we are young and a desire to explore all the things around us. We also have a desire to wonder why we exist. When we attend church and are taught, as children, the stories of the Bible, we have a desire to find out why God created us and what our purpose is in this life. Our reaction then is to look at the bigger picture. From a biblical perspective, man does have a greater purpose on earth. When we realize that we were created by God for the benefit of one another and to serve his purpose, we have a responsibility to fulfill our individual destiny.

An example of this in the Bible is in Matthew 19:14, "But Jesus said, 'Suffer little children, and forbid them not, to come unto me: for of such is the kingdom of heaven.'"

He is calling on us to be humble and have faith to believe. In 1 Peter 3:15, it says, "But in your hearts revere Christ as Lord. Always be prepared to give an answer to everyone who asks you to give the reason for the hope that you have." When the Bible talks about being like a child, it does not mean that we should not be educated and have reasons for our beliefs. Having faith like a child means we should have confidence in the promises of Christ and faith even in situations where we cannot see the outcome.

Skeptics generally abandon their old thought patterns as they learn new truths about the Bible and its teachings. In a sense, secular education leads us away from God, but faith and study of the Scriptures lead us to Christ. Many abandon their faith when they are systematically taught that there is no rational reason to believe in God. However, many are strengthened in their faith when they attend church and seek God with all their heart. The Bible commands us to make disciples of all men, which simply means a follower of Christ. We do this by teaching them the Scriptures and allowing them to make a choice.

Other religions in contrast

The atheist would say that there is no God because religion is flawed and imperfect, and there is no proof that God exists. Religion is not the answer to eternal salvation. The agnostic would say that you cannot prove God through the rational mind. Intellectualism is not the answer to spiritual enlightenment. Mormonism teaches that there are many gods in existence and that you can become a god.

Islam teaches that Jesus is not God in the flesh but just a prophet and not God. Some religions teach that we reincarnate while others do not. Some teach there is hell, and others do not. They cannot all be true. If they cannot all be true, it cannot be true that all religions lead to God. So why should we believe in Christ? Christianity teaches that there is only one God and that he sent his son, Jesus, to die for our sins, and he was raised from the dead. Salvation is offered to all through Jesus Christ and him alone.

Christ's resurrection

Within Christianity, the resurrection is vitally important. Without the resurrection, our faith is useless (1 Corinthians 15:14). It was Jesus's resurrection that changed the lives of the disciples. After Jesus was crucified, the disciples ran and hid. But when they saw the risen Lord, they knew that what Jesus had said and done proved that he was, indeed, God in the flesh, the Savior.

No other religious leader had died in full view of trained executioners, had a guarded tomb, and then had risen three days later to appear to many people. This resurrection is proof of who Jesus is and that he did accomplish what he set out to do: provide the only means of redemption for humanity.

Buddha did not rise from the dead, Muhammad did not rise from the dead, Confucius did not rise from the dead, Krishna did not rise from the dead, etc. Only Jesus had physically risen from the dead, walked on water, claimed to be God, and raised others from the dead. He had conquered death. Why trust anyone else? Why trust anyone who can be held by physical death when we have a Messiah who is greater than death itself?

Why should anyone trust in Christianity over Islam, Buddhism, Mormonism, or anything else? It is because there are absolute truths. Only in Christianity are there accurately fulfilled prophecies of a coming Messiah. Only in Christianity do we have the extremely accurate transmission of the eyewitness documents (Gospels). So we can trust what was originally written. Only in Christianity do we have the person of Christ who claimed to be God, who performed many miracles to prove his claim of divinity, who died and rose from the dead, and who said that he alone was the way, the truth, and the life (John 14:6). All this adds to the legitimacy and credibility of Christianity above all other religions—all based on the person of Jesus.

The Scriptures and historians account the resurrection of Christ—that he was buried, that he was raised on the third day according to the Scriptures, and that he appeared to Cephas (Peter), and then to the Twelve. After that, he appeared to more than five hundred of the brothers and sisters at the same time, most of who are still living, though some have fallen asleep. Then he appeared to James, then to all the apostles, and last of all he appeared to me (Paul) also, as to one abnormally born. (1 Corinthians 15:4–8)

The Bible says that over five hundred people saw Jesus ascend into heaven after his resurrection. He spent forty days on earth after he was raised from the dead teaching his disciples. He then returned to heaven from where he came and sent the Holy Spirit to men so that they would be empowered to serve him. The evidence was overwhelming: Christ was raised from the dead just as he said. The disciples were converted from skeptics to people who would lay down their life for Christ.

God cares for all of us and desires that all mankind turn to him for salvation. I think people were and are drawn to the mercy of Jesus. Jesus was not like the other religious leaders. The other religious leaders paid their alms to the poor and preached their sermons and taught their religious studies, all while they looked down their noses at everybody who didn't measure up to their standards of righteousness. They performed religious duties and lived according to religious laws, but there was no life in it. Their teaching oppressed people. It beat them down. It left them in despair. But Jesus was different. He wasn't filled with coldhearted religion; he was filled with mercy. He hung out with hated tax collectors, prostitutes, sinners, and the sick. He died for the lawyer just like he died for the drug addict. No matter what you have done or whether you lived a life with high moral standards, he died for the religious, the intellectual, as well as the faithless. He is truly a God who saves. This is the message we are commanded to take to the ends of the earth.

And Jesus came up and spoke to them, saying, "All authority has been given to Me in heaven and on earth. Go therefore and make disciples of all the nations, baptizing them in the name of the Father and the Son and the Holy Spirit, teaching them to observe all that I commanded you; and lo,

I am with you always, even to the end of the age." (Matthew 28:18–20)

This passage of Scripture we all know as the Great Commission. But what does it mean in our lives right now? This verse is our purpose and our calling as Christians. It is a commandment from our Savior about how we should be living every day. Within this one commandment, there are distinct points about the purpose we have been given and how we are to grow God's kingdom.

Go and make disciples

Some of us will have the opportunity to serve God in foreign countries. But most of us will serve God here in our own country. We don't have to go to a far-off land to follow the Great Commission. Wherever we are and whatever we are doing, it is our responsibility to tell people about Jesus. We can't leave it to chance that someone else will do it for us. God puts us where he wants us to be, and we can win souls for him right here in our own backyards. All we have to do is look around us, and we will see that there are so many people who are already in our lives who need Jesus. Whether it is our calling to serve God at home or abroad, we have been given the power of the Holy Spirit to fulfill our purpose to make disciples.

"But you shall receive power when the Holy Spirit has come upon you; and you shall be witnesses to Me in Jerusalem, and in all Judea and Samaria, and to the end of the earth" (Acts 1:8).

About the Author

Richard H. Crowder is a businessman, entrepreneur, pastor, and founder of United Faith Ministries. He earned a master of divinity degree, received an honorary doctor of divinity degree for his work in the ministry and community, and earned a doctor of ministerial studies degree. His years of teaching and speaking and writing sermons prompted him to write more about the topic to reach a broader audience.

Milton Keynes UK
Ingram Content Group UK Ltd.
UKHW011539310124
437030UK00001B/76